All about
GROWING
for your
FREEZER

Violet Stevenson
(Growing)

Mary Norwak
(Freezing)

Hamlyn
London · New York · Sydney · Toronto

Acknowledgements

Line drawings by Val Biro
Cover photograph by Eric Carter
We would like to thank the following for
providing the photographs used in this book:
Amateur Gardening, Elly Arnstein, Pat Brindley,
John Cowley, Robert Corbin, Ernest Crowson,
Brian Furner, The Harry Smith Horticultural
Photographic Collection and Sutton and Sons Ltd.

First published in 1977 by
The Hamlyn Publishing Group Limited
London · New York · Sydney · Toronto
Astronaut House, Feltham, Middlesex, England

Filmset in England by Filmtype Services Ltd, Scarborough,
in 10 on 11 pt. Monophoto Baskerville
Printed in England by Hazell Watson & Viney Ltd, Aylesbury

Contents

Part 1 How to grow and freeze

Introduction 4

Growing vegetables 5
What to grow 5
Soil preparation 8
Seed sowing and aftercare 11

Freezing vegetables 15
Planning for the freezer 15
Blanching 15
Open freezing 16
Packaging 16
Thawing and cooking 16
High quality storage life 17

Growing fruit 17
What to grow 17
Soil preparation 20
Planting 20

Freezing fruit 20
Preparing the fruit 20
Dry unsweetened pack 21
Sugar pack 21
Syrup pack 21
Purée 21
Thawing and cooking 21

Part 2 Vegetables

Artichokes 24

Asparagus 25

Beans 28

Beet 36

Broccoli 40

Brussels sprouts 44

Red cabbage 44

Capsicum 45

Carrots 48

Cauliflower 49

Celery 52

Courgettes and marrows 53

Leeks 56

Peas 57

Potatoes 60

Spinach 64

Sweet corn 64

Tomatoes 65

Part 3 Fruit

Apples 67

Blackberries 68

Cherries 69

Currants 70

Gooseberries 72

Peaches and nectarines 72

Pears 74

Plums and gages 75

Raspberries 77

Rhubarb 78

Strawberries 79

Part 1
How to grow and freeze

Anyone who can grow any kind of plant can grow some for eating and at the same time experience the pleasure of tasting the full flavour of fresh fruit and vegetables – incomparable with those which have to be bought from the shop.

The larger the garden, the greater the harvest one can expect to gather, but even a small plot can become a highly productive area if the gardener selects the plants wisely. However, it might not be generally recognized that any garden, and especially the little one which serves a small family, can become so much more productive by using a freezer to store surplus fruits and vegetables, picked at the peak of their perfection. Nor might it be known that there are many varieties of several kinds of vegetable which have been especially bred for the freezer.

It is possible by careful planning to ensure not only a bountiful harvest, but also a succession of fresh vegetables and fruits at certain seasons of the year. However, even carefully laid plans have to bend to natural conditions and sometimes there are gluts when a crop matures all at the same time. Here the freezer comes to the gardener's aid. It also helps you to make more room available for crops at the seasons in which they grow fastest. As soon as they are at their peak, some rows of vegetables can be cleared quickly instead of little by little as they are required. This means that they occupy space for the minimum length of time. Now that land is at such a premium, there should be no wasted space, no long intervals during the best growing times when row space lies fallow.

This book endeavours to demonstrate how rewarding it can be to grow food crops and how the task is doubly rewarding if the gardener also appreciates that the freezer can be an extension of the garden.

4

Growing vegetables

What to grow

Some plants do better on some soils and in some areas than others and this is just as true about those that are classified as vegetables and fruits as it is for the more decorative kinds. It follows, therefore, that if you select the best kinds for your garden you will gain the greatest value from them.

The type of soil is important and so is climate. It may be necessary to feed and cultivate to improve the first and to provide protection in some way to control the second. Many of our most prolific summer vegetables – French and runner beans, the marrow family, sweet corn and tomatoes, for example – are dependent on warm nights and generally fair weather as well as adequate water supplies. These crops should not be planted outdoors in the open until all danger of spring frost is past. After this they have to be encouraged to grow quickly and to mature early so that all can be harvested before the cold nights of autumn set in. This means that if you hope to grow them, you have either to find some source from which you can buy well-grown plants ready to go out at the proper time, or you have to provide some means of raising them in heat yourself, in a frost-free (that is, a 'cold') greenhouse, in a

With the aid of a freezer, a harvest of vegetables can be enjoyed out of season

Dwarf French beans can be sown successionally to prolong cropping

warmed frame or on sunny windowsills in a warm home. Once planted they need to grow fast, so soil should be rich and retentive of moisture. It is worth taking some trouble over these crops simply because they are so prolific once they are growing well. All will provide good freezer stores.

It is possible to sow the seed of these summer vegetables in the open ground, but as you would expect, the plants come into production a little later. This being the case, northern gardeners and those in cold areas would be wise to make an early start.

By using different varieties at different times of the year, most of the hardy plants such as cabbage, lettuce, onions, spinach and even cauliflowers, can be grown in such a way that they provide a continuous supply of fresh produce. This being the case there is no need, except in time of gluts, to consider freezing them, but some others such as Brussels sprouts, broccoli and sometimes cauliflower and spinach are available at certain seasons only.

Most root vegetables, beet, carrot and parsnips for instance, are grown to maturity and lifted and stored in the autumn for use during winter and early spring, by which time they usually begin sprouting. Because these store so well, some people believe that it is not worth while freezing root vegetables, but there are other considerations to be taken into account. In the first place you do not *have* to eat old, matured vegetables. By freezing them you can have tasty, tender, young vegetables the year round and not just at the beginning of the season. But more important, I think, is that by growing quick, early roots it is possible to gain more garden space.

These crops occupy the space of a row for a matter of weeks rather than months, especially if you can give them a little cloche protection. Usually the whole row can be cleared very quickly since growth is uniform. The space the plants occupied can then be immediately used for some other crop, either long-standing winter greens or some other quick-maturing summer crop such as lettuce or late-sown peas.

If this method is followed, suit-able varieties of root vegetables should be chosen; for instance, quick-maturing or forcing varieties of carrots instead of the long, large, maincrop varieties, and little round beetroots instead of the long, large roots. These beet can make amends for their lack of size not only because they are of such superior flavour but also because their leaves can be saved and frozen like any other leaf beet, seakale or perpetual beet, for instance.

This concept of using the freezer to get more from the garden sometimes means that one should break away from the traditional ways and adopt methods which better suit the situation. For instance, in order to create a continuous supply of peas it is the practice to plant more than one type, that is, early, maincrop and late, and there are special varieties for this purpose. But if you find that one type suits your purposes or your garden better than another (you may have a late garden in which case maincrops are better than earlies) it would be best to grow plenty of this one type rather than follow the successional method. Keep in

mind, though, that if they mature all at once they will also have to be prepared for freezing all at once. One point worth mentioning—since the early crops mature quite quickly, their ground is not occupied for such a long period as it would be if the successional crops were grown.

Although there is not the same seasonal diversity with the dwarf French beans, these are often sown at intervals in order to prolong the crop of fresh pods. However, if you are growing them mainly for freezing, here again it might be best to sow or plant several rows at one time: single rows are often wasteful of space. If you have a little garden you can save a considerable amount of room by planting beans quite close together, with 15 cm (6 in) between the plants, in a block of three or four rows. If you make two or more blocks, you need only a narrow picking path between each block.

Another good way of using the freezer to stretch garden space is in late spring when certain crops are still in the ground. Nothing is more wasteful than the half rows or half-picked plants which remain at this season. If you wait for them all to be used, you are losing space and season. Leeks, parsnips, spinach, leaf beet, and broccoli can be cleared to make way for new crops.

Obviously, the vegetables to produce are those which you like and use most, those which are the most expensive to buy in the shops and those you like but which are only occasionally on sale. Choice is bound to be a personal matter, but it is worth pointing out that there is seldom a dearth of the everyday, traditional vegetables because these are commercially produced in such great quantities. If your garden is very small it may not really be economical to grow such things as cabbages and swedes or even onions; fill it with

the less common kinds. It is worth planning crops. It might pay you, for instance, to concentrate on expensive salads and herbs in winter and complement these with summer vegetables from your freezer.

Tomatoes, a wonderful stand-by, are available all the year round, but the price asked in winter often prohibits them for use in anything but salads. Cheaper frozen tomatoes, juice and purées, will prove to be most valuable to cooks the whole year round.

It is worth studying seed catalogues carefully before deciding what variety of each vegetable to grow. An old, familiar variety may not be the best choice. Although it is possible to freeze any of the vegetables mentioned in

this book, some varieties of these vegetables really do freeze better than others. For example, peas recommended for freezing have a higher sugar content than other varieties of pea; beans remain firmer and greener, corn is more tender, broccoli less likely to disintegrate. On the other hand, it is comforting to know that a glut of vegetables need not go to waste. The freezer will take care of them until you are ready to use them.

The most profitable vegetables, especially for a small garden, are the cut-and-come-again kinds. Although some cabbages will sprout again after the heart is cut and will then give greens rather than hearts, generally speaking once the heart is cut the plant is worthless and should be thrown out to make room for a new crop. On the other hand, a bush-type courgette, marrow or squash, a tomato or a tripod of runner beans will occupy no more space than a large cabbage and will yield a succession of fruits. As a rule all the highly productive summer vegetables can be harvested daily.

Left: Runner beans are especially rewarding, yielding a high return for the space they occupy
Below: Tomatoes are easy to raise in a growing bag which is supplied already filled with a formulated compost

Soil preparation

If vegetables are to be tender they must be encouraged to grow quickly. The longer they take to reach maturity the tougher and smaller they will be. This means that they have to be provided with all their needs, indulged in fact. They must have access to the plant foods they need and to adequate water. Some crops, celery for instance, need much more water than others and it is necessary to apply water to these even if the soil is already moist and rich enough to carry the other crops without artificial watering. Well-cultivated soil should be water retentive, although in time of drought even this may become dry. The plant foods lie in the soil and some soils are naturally richer than others. Fortunately, plants can be fed as well as watered, but ideally the soil should be prepared or cultivated so that it is in 'good heart'. This means that it is rich with bacteria, which will break down the nutrients into a form that the plants can easily absorb.

Gardeners who have already grown flowers in their plots will have a pretty good idea of the kind of soil they are dealing with. Soils vary in different parts of the country and there are plants adapted to the different soil types. In most cases it is easy to see whether a soil is sandy, chalky, peaty or consisting of clay. And these soils fit into another category, being light, medium or heavy. Ordinary soil, fortunately the most common in gardens, is fairly well balanced, being neither more of one thing nor another.

All soil needs humus, which is decayed organic matter. It helps to hold moisture, it aerates the soil and keeps it both warm and cool. It is high in bacterial content, processing raw chemicals into foods which roots can absorb. Soil which has been culti-

vated for a long time is often deficient in humus and is known as 'starved' soil. On the other hand, maiden soil, which has not carried cultivated crops, is often rich in humus and when made into a new vegetable garden will give bumper crops.

The condition and richness of a soil is very dependent upon its texture. Clay soil, for example, is compacted with poor aeration and sandy soil is too aerated. The first tends to remain cold, wet and sticky, the second dry and hot. It is possible, even simple, to im-

prove soil textures. Lime helps heavy soils to become crumbly and any kind of organic fibrous material dug into clay soils, such as peat, well-rotted animal manures and home-made compost will help to make it open and aerated. The same materials worked into sandy soils will help them to retain moisture, which indicates their importance in the

Making a compost heap. (1) Vegetable refuse, grass cuttings and fallen leaves can be added. (2) Applying a compost accelerator to hasten decomposition.

1

2

vegetable gardening scene.

All gardeners are well advised to make a compost heap, for this is a cheap and bountiful source of humus. Use all your vegetable refuse for the heap and add to it grass cuttings and fallen leaves. You will be wise, though, not to include diseased vegetables and foliage; these are better burned. A metre (yard) square of ground

(3) The heap should be kept moist. (4) When the pile is about 1 to 1·5 m (4 to 5 ft) high, it should be finished off with a layer of soil

will suffice. Mark it out, firm the ground and on it pile the material to be composted so that it too is firm and neat. Tread or beat it down with the back of a spade. When the pile is about 15 cm thick (6 in) sprinkle it with one of the proprietary activators to help the refuse decompose quickly, or use sulphate of ammonia and superphosphate, 1·5 g ($\frac{1}{2}$ oz) of each to every square metre (square yard) of surface. Sprinkle the heap with water, about 5 litres (1 gal) to every square metre (square yard)

of surface. Cover the heap with a 5-cm (2-in) thick layer of soil and continue the process until another 15 cm layer is ready to be treated, and so on until the heap is about 1 to 1·5 m (4 to 5 ft) high. In summer water the heap about once a week. When it is stacked, turn the heap over, transferring the outside to the middle so that it rots evenly all through. When the compost has rotted properly it will look like a good crumbly soil and will be pleasant to handle.

You can buy mesh or plastic containers for compost heaps to keep them neat. It is a good plan to buy two and place them side by side. Fill one first, and then turn it by emptying it into the empty bin, moving the outside of the heap to the warm, 'cooked' underside.

This compost will provide a wonderful method of rejuvenating the soil as well as improving its texture and character. If your soil is very alkaline, chalky or sandy, make seed drills and planting holes a little deeper or wider than recommended and line them with compost. Sow the seed on this at the recommended depth, cover lightly with a little more compost and top with a little of the natural soil. After you have done this a few times you will find that all the soil, not just that in the drills, is improving. The worm population should also increase and this will help to improve soil texture.

Peaty soils are acid soils. Some are so acid that only certain plants can tolerate them, and few vegetables are among them. Most acid soils can be corrected by adding lime, but this should be used with caution because it is possible to apply too much, even to very acid soils.

You can buy soil testing kits or send soil samples to your County Horticultural Adviser, to the Royal Horticultural Society or to one of the several major garden

3

4

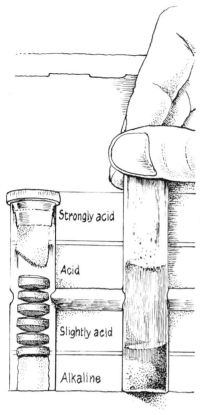

Strongly acid

Acid

Slightly acid

Alkaline

chemical manufacturers. Neutral soils have a pH value of 7·0, with acid soils giving a reading below this and alkaline soils above. Soils which indicate below pH 5·5 or above pH 8·0 will not produce healthy crops or perhaps will give no crops at all and will need to be corrected.

Only few vegetables like a really limy or chalky soil with a high pH, but many, especially brassicas or the cabbage family, need a certain amount of lime if they are to grow well. Guidance on this point will be given later when dealing specifically with individual crops. Allow an interval of at least six weeks after applying either lime or manure before applying the other, since one tends to counteract the benefits of the other.

Well-rotted manures and com-

Preparing the ground. The soil should be thoroughly dug over. Manure or garden compost is forked in to the bottom of each trench

10

posts are important because they stimulate essential bacterial activity in soils, without which plants cannot easily absorb the plant foods present. These organic substances do not actually hold much plant food, which is why inorganic fertilizers are used in addition, in order to boost a plant's performance. These fertilizers should not be used if rich humus-making materials are absent, or in time the soil is likely to suffer. Some vegetables are better helped by artificials than others. It is possible to buy balanced fertilizers which contain the chemicals most necessary to plant growth, that is, nitrogen or some nitrogenous material, phosphates, potash and certain trace elements.

Before beginning to make a vegetable garden, the soil should be well dug and enriched. Make the edges neat so that crops can be carried right up to the boundaries. If the plot borders on to grass, keep the edge clipped so that the grass does not invade the vegetable area and require weeding. If the plot is cut into rough grass, weedkiller applied to a narrow margin all the way round the perimeter of the plot keeps weeds from encroaching.

If possible, do any necessary digging before the bad weather sets in, not so much for your own comfort but so that the elements can work on the soil and render it malleable in spring. Soil which has been left in rough clods and exposed to wind, rain and frost will crumble in spring at the touch of a rake. You will then be able to work the rake back and forth to produce a fine, level tilth, the ideal medium for seed sowing.

Work the soil only when it is dry or slightly moist. If it sticks to the sole of your shoe it is too wet and should not be walked on or it will pan and cake badly. Everything possible should be done to keep the tilth in perfect condition.

Seed sowing and aftercare

Most seeds are sown in drills, which are shallow furrows drawn in the soil by a hoe or sharp stick, the depth of the drill depending on the type of seed and the kind of vegetable. Seed should never be sown deeply unless specifically directed. As a very general rule the seed needs to be covered by about twice its own depth with soil. If the drill is too shallow the wind may uncover the seed or it may be washed out by heavy rain.

To save space, seeds are sown in straight rows, and these should run from north to south. Use a garden line as a guide. Push in the end supports until the line rests on the soil and then, standing on the line to keep it straight, draw the drill along one side of it.

When half-hardy plants such as sweet corn and courgettes are sown directly into the soil it is advisable to make special preparation for them, not only so that the soil shall be rich, but also that it shall be warm. You can mark where the plants are to grow and then remove some of the soil and replace it with a better mixture. Alternatively, you can take out a deeper hole and line it with fresh lawn mowings which will generate heat, topped with well-rotted compost or manure, and covered with soil or peat. The seeds will then have cosy bottom heat. Cloches placed over the soil a week or so before the seed is sown will also help to warm it.

Drawing out a seed drill with the aid of a hoe and garden line. The depth of the drill depends on the type of seed

(1) Seeds may be sown in a nursery bed and transplanted when large enough to handle. (2) Planting out seedlings in their final quarters. (3) Watering in newly planted seedlings

Most of the vegetable seeds are sown where the plants are to mature and the seedlings are thinned out rather than transplanted, although this is not, as we shall see, a hard-and-fast rule. Some seeds are sown in a special place set apart, a nursery bed, and transplanted either on to another part of this bed or to their final places when they are large enough to handle.

Seeds need moisture before they will germinate, but it is not good, nor is it easy, to sow seeds in wet soil. The day should be fine but not windy. In very dry weather it is advisable to make the drill and soak it thoroughly before sowing the seed, but it is best to wait until after a shower and then to sow when the soil has dried to the right consistency. If germination does not take place quickly, seeds tend to disappear for one reason or another.

While most vegetable seeds can be sown in a long row across the plot, even in the area where they are to mature, in some cases it is more economical in seed, time and trouble to start them off in a special nursery bed and then to transplant them in the bed and finally move them out to their permanent stations. Apart from anything else, they can be germinating and growing here while the more productive area is being used to the full.

A nursery bed need not be far from the main growing area: indeed, it can be made in one section of it. A strip along the side of the path is often the most convenient place. It is best to make a raised bed because this is better drained besides being warmer than a flat soil surface. Make it roughly the shape of an up-turned roasting tin. About 1 m (1 yd) wide is a good size, and as long as you need. The rows should be made across the width. It is best sited in a place which gets a little shade but which is not actually shady all day. If no shade is available, provide a little for the young seedlings by

pushing in a few peasticks or a piece of mesh on the sunny side.

If you are troubled by sparrows or other birds which eat young seedlings, or by cats scratching up the fine soil, you can protect the seeds and seedlings and give them shade at the same time by folding a piece of small-mesh

Regular hoeing between the rows will keep weeds under control

Thinning carrots. These young carrots are excellent for freezing

wire netting down the centre to make a tent-shaped piece long enough to cover one or two entire rows. Close the ends. If you sow your seeds early in the year, as advised for lettuce for instance, you can stand a cloche on the bed, but make the bed a little wider than the cloche so that it sits on it firmly.

A layer of John Innes seed soil mixture on the surface of the prepared bed will give your seedlings a good healthy start. Sow your seed into this mixture and cover them with it too. You will find few, if any, weeds and really healthy seedlings.

Rows across the garden are almost certain to need a line as a guide, but those on a nursery bed are likely to be much shorter and in this case a rake handle can be used, marked if required in centimetre or foot measurements. To make a short seed drill, lay the rake flat on the prepared soil and draw the drill along the side of the rake handle, using the angle of the head and the handle as a set square to ensure the drills are straight.

Always mark drills at both ends

Pricking out seedlings which have been sown in boxes under glass

by pushing a short cane into the ground before the seeds are sown and measure the distance between the rows by these guide sticks. Try to sow thinly, bearing in mind that each seed is a potential plant.

Not all seeds to be transplanted later go into a nursery bed; some thinnings can be transplanted from the long rows. Usually these mature a little later because their growth has received a check and this is a simple way of creating a succession. Dwarf French beans, for instance, can be sown at 7 to 8-cm (3-in) intervals and later alternate plants can be lifted and transferred to another row 15 cm (6 in) apart. The same is true of lettuces, some cabbages, Swiss chard and leeks, to mention a few.

It is not practical to replant thinnings of root crops such as carrot, parsnip and turnip. They would probably grow all right, but instead of a well-shaped root you would find it divided and misshapen.

How you sow the seeds is really up to you, but I find that the simplest way to sow small seeds is carefully to open the packet, fold the flap at the centre so that it makes a little chute and then to sift the seed into the drill. There is always a tendency to sow too thickly.

Wait until the seedlings have made true leaves before beginning to thin them, and even then thin them out by stages rather than in one fell swoop. This covers you against accidents, such as depredation by slugs or birds or some other minor tragedy.

Some roots such as carrot and beet can be pulled young and others left to mature. In this case you should first thin them so that there is only 2 cm (1 in) or so between the plants. When they are large enough pull alternate roots for eating and continue this way until there is a good space between those which are to remain in the row until autumn.

Thin seedlings after a shower, once the soil is dry enough to walk on. In times of drought water the row an hour or so beforehand.

If you intend to transplant the seedlings see that their roots are disturbed as little as possible and that they come up with plenty of soil adhering to them. Prise them up with a handfork, separate and lift them by holding their leaves. Lift only a very few at a time and do not leave their roots exposed to the air. Make a planting hole with a trowel and line it with rotted compost or moist peat. Insert the seedling, holding it by its leaves as you cover the roots and pressing these down firmly but gently. Do not bury the seed leaves or cotyledons. These should be just above the soil after planting as they were before lifting.

Some plants are just too tender to be sown in the garden in early spring and these are usually raised in heat or under glass. This means that the seed is sown thinly in boxes of seed soil. When the seedlings are large enough to handle they are gently prised up with their roots as intact as possible and transplanted 5 to 8 cm (2 to 3 in) each way in another box, or alternatively into soil or peat blocks or small individual pots. This process is known as pricking off or pricking out, possibly because such a small hole is needed for the little roots. A pencil makes a good dibber.

Freezing vegetables

It is most important to freeze produce quickly after harvesting. Vegetables become stale and the quality deteriorates rapidly, so it is best to pick small quantities and process them at once rather than wait until you have a sackful on the kitchen table. Vegetables for freezing should be small and tender, but if there is some variation in age and size, grade the produce before processing. In this way, you get even blanching and freezing, and it is also easier to time later cooking. Wash all vegetables thoroughly in cold water, grade and cut, if necessary, before processing.

Planning for the freezer

Just a few vegetables do not freeze well, but are obviously needed in the garden. Leafy salad vegetables (such as lettuce) and radishes do not freeze well. Carrots can be frozen when young, but the large older ones are best left in the garden or stored elsewhere. Turnips and other roots also stand well in the garden, and so do cabbages, so it is rarely worth wasting freezer space on them. Fully grown marrows store well in a dry place, but courgettes and very young marrows can be frozen. Leeks and celery stand through the winter, but a few bags of each are worth freezing

for summer use, when their delicate flavour is valuable for soups. Therefore, plan to use the freezer space for real family favourites like peas and beans, for exotics like asparagus, artichokes and sweetcorn, and for small quantities of culinary treasures such as leeks and tomatoes.

Blanching

It is very important that vegetables are blanched (cooked for a short time in boiling water) to stop the working of the enzymes which affect flavour, colour and nutritive value in the freezer. It is possible to store unblanched vegetables in the freezer for up to three months, but the quality deteriorates very rapidly after that time, and it is a pity to waste good produce by lazy freezing.

Vegetables should be prepared and frozen as soon as possible after picking

Open freezing

For a quantity of vegetables, the fast-freeze control should be switched on about 3 hours beforehand until a temperature of $-28°C$ ($-18°F$) is achieved. Spread the blanched, chilled vegetables on to baking sheets or freezer trays, and freeze in the fast-freeze compartment until hard. Tip into bags or rigid containers and the vegetables will remain separate and free-flowing.

Packaging

Most vegetables can be packed in polythene bags. If they are delicate and likely to be bruised (for example, asparagus, broccoli), pack them in rigid containers, and alternate the heads to avoid damage.

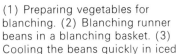

(1) Preparing vegetables for blanching. (2) Blanching runner beans in a blanching basket. (3) Cooling the beans quickly in iced water. (4) Blanched vegetables, well drained and packed for freezing in polythene bags or rigid containers

Before blanching, make sure you have plenty of ice. You need at least a bucketful to chill a few pounds of vegetables, because tap water is just not cold enough to do the job properly with the result that vegetables continue cooking after blanching and become flabby and poorly coloured.

For successful blanching, use a large saucepan with a lid, which holds at least 4·5 litres (8 pints) of water comfortably. You will also need a wire blanching basket or salad basket to hold the vegetables together.

Before blanching, get a bowl of water and ice with a colander standing in the bowl, and a timer or watch with a second hand. Only blanch 450 g (1 lb) vegetables at a time, and time the

blanching and cooling very carefully, or the vegetables will lose their colour and texture.

Bring 4·5 lites (8 pints) of water to the boil. Put the vegetables in the basket and cover with a lid. Bring the water to the boil again as quickly as possible, and start timing immediately the water bubbles. As soon as the time is up, tip the vegetables into the colander standing in the ice-chilled water. Cooling time should be exactly the same as for blanching. Drain thoroughly before open freezing or packing. With care, it is possible to blanch one lot of vegetables while another lot is cooling, so that a quantity of produce can be prepared in a matter of minutes. The same water can be used for several batches.

Packaging materials for freezing — polythene bags and containers, labels, ties and sealer tape

Thawing and cooking

Vegetables should not be thawed before cooking, except for corn-on-the-cob which will not cook thoroughly from the frozen state. A solid block of spinach is also difficult to deal with, and can be partly thawed before the final heating. Only use about 150 ml

($\frac{1}{4}$ pint) water to cook 450 g (1 lb) vegetables, and cook for the minimum of time as the vegetables have already been partly cooked during blanching.

One or two vegetables, such as new potatoes and runner beans, are better if not directly exposed to water during the final cooking after freezing. They are best frozen in boil-in-bags which later can be plunged into boiling water for cooking.

High quality storage life

Most vegetables can be stored for 12 months in the freezer, but it is important to use them regularly as storage space is expensive. There is little point in keeping produce the full twelve months, or there will be no anticipation of the fresh seasonal vegetables. The ideal is to go on using summer's vegetables until about February, supplemented by roots and greens, until the first varieties of spring vegetables begin to appear.

In order to keep freezer stock properly and see that it is used in rotation, all packages must be labelled with the date of freezing. All vegetables of the same kind should be kept together in a basket or large batching-bag, or on a shelf. A simple record of the varieties and quantities of each vegetable will enable you to know when stocks are beginning to run down, and when less popular vegetables might be introduced to the family diet so they can be used up.

Growing fruit

What to grow

The pleasant thing about most fruit plants is that they are decorative as well as useful. Individual trees can be used to grace a garden, even as a superlative specimen on a lawn, so long as it is of the right variety and needs no others of its kind nearby to pollinate it. Fruit trees can be used as screens and boundaries. Many, dwarf pyramid apples and pears for instance, can be planted quite close together, just 4 ft apart. Some can cover walls, or be trained up and over paths and walks as pergolas or even made into arbours – an attractive way of saving garden space. They can be grown as espaliers or cordons alongside a path, used to hide boundary wires and to furnish inside walls of fruit cages.

Apples grown as cordons make a useful screen or boundary fence

Below: Blanching vegetables — cooking them for a few moments in boiling water — ensures that they will remain in top condition while frozen

Right: Globe artichokes should be blanched and frozen immediately they are picked as they soon lose their freshness

Apart from this, there are many places, even in the smallest garden, where fruit can be grown quite well. A row of raspberries can be screened by a rock garden or a herbaceous border. Alpine strawberries make an attractive and fruitful edging to a path in partial shade. Blackcurrants will grow in the shade of larger trees. Cordons of currants and gooseberries need not be grown in straight rows; they can be planted in circles where they can be pruned and picked easily. Even rhubarb is a handsome plant and can be brought to the fore to share the limelight with other ornamentals.

Soil preparation

Since most trees and bushes are likely to be in the ground for a long time and are expected to crop heavily once they begin, the soil should be prepared thoroughly. It should be well drained and deep—fruit tree roots spread deep and wide. Most fruits thrive on slightly acid soils, but not on the very acid kinds, which should be adjusted. Most stone fruits, however, need a little lime in the soil. It is advisable to make soil tests and also to seek the nurseryman's advice on varieties most suited to your local conditions.

Soil which has already been cultivated and manured is the best for fruit. Otherwise, dig uncultivated land well and as far ahead of planting as possible. Add both humusy materials and fertilizers.

Planting

The possibility of damage from frost, which may kill blossom, and wind, which damages the fruit, should be taken into account when planning the site. Where there is a choice, sloping ground is best.

Fruit grows best in full sun, which is why most wall-trained plants should face south or west. Only few do well on a north-facing wall. East walls are likely to get full morning sun which damages blossom after a frosty night and so should not be used.

Planting is best done in late autumn or during winter, so long as the weather is 'open', which means that no planting should be attempted when the soil is frosted or sodden. Container-grown specimens can be planted at any time of the year provided the ground is in suitable condition, and bearing in mind that young plants will need regular watering if the weather is dry.

Freezing fruit

Preparing the fruit

Carefully prepared fruit will freeze well and taste freshly picked, but full-flavoured fruit, such as berries, gives the best results. Top-quality fruit should be frozen when perfectly ripe, and must be processed as soon as possible after picking. As with vegetables, it is better to process small quantities at a time. All fruit should be washed in ice-chilled water to make it firm and avoid juice loss, and then must be well drained. Fruit may be frozen dry and unsweetened, or mixed with sugar, or in syrup, or made into purée. Fruit may be open frozen before packing, and this is particularly suitable for berries which crush easily.

Dry unsweetened pack

This is a useful way to freeze fruit, as it can then be used for sugar-free diets as well as for all types of pies, puddings and jams. This method is not suitable for fruit which discolours badly, as sugar helps to retard the action of the enzymes which cause darkening. Pack in polythene bags or rigid containers in 225-g (8-oz), 450-g (1-lb) or 1-kg (2-lb) packs and label carefully. When making jam later, allow 10 per cent more fruit than the recipe, as there is a slight pectin loss in the freezer.

Sugar pack

Soft, juicy fruit can be packed in dry sugar, and this is also good for sliced fruit such as apples. Allow about 450 g (1 lb) sugar to each 1·5 kg (3 lb) fruit and mix the fruit and sugar together, or arrange them in layers, topping with a layer of sugar. This method of packing may produce too much sweetness for some palates, and the fruit is not so suitable for recipe use later. Sugar also draws the fruit juices, and can result in mushiness after thawing of fruit such as strawberries.

Syrup pack

Uncooked fruit can be frozen in sugar syrup, and this is good for non-juicy fruit and fruit which discolours easily. The syrup should be made with white sugar and water (brown sugar colours the fruit, and honey affects the flavour). The sugar should be dissolved in the water, brought to the boil, then cooled before use. Fruit in syrup should be packed in rigid containers, leaving a headspace to allow for expansion. This space should be filled with crumpled greaseproof paper or freezer paper to prevent the fruit rising above the syrup and discolouring. A little ascorbic acid,

obtainable from the chemist, can be added to prevent discoloration, or a little lemon juice may be used.

There are three main syrup strengths used in freezing fruit:
30 per cent syrup (light) –
200 g (7 oz) sugar 600 ml (1 pint) water
40 per cent syrup (medium) –
300 g (11 oz) sugar 600 ml (1 pint) water
50 per cent syrup (heavy) –
450 g (16 oz) sugar 600 ml (1 pint) water

Purée

Fruit purée is useful in the freezer as it takes up little space, and can be quickly made into fools, mousses, ices or sauces when thawed. It is also useful for making the best of slightly damaged or over-ripe fruit. Plums, apples, gooseberries and currants need cooking in a little water before being sieved into purée, but raspberries, strawberries and blackberries may be sieved without cooking.

Freezing pears in a syrup pack. Note the crumpled greaseproof paper holding the fruit down to prevent it from discolouring

Thawing and cooking

Fruit is best thawed slowly in the refrigerator and eaten while still slightly frozen. It quickly deteriorates in quality and flavour if left to stand after thawing. It is best to keep the packs closed during thawing to prevent discoloration. Allow about 6 hours per $\frac{1}{2}$ kg (1 lb) for the fruit to thaw completely in the refrigerator; purée will thaw in about 4 hours. Frozen fruit may be put into hot sugar syrup and poached carefully so the fruit does not break up.

Left: Swiss Chard, or seakale beet, has a long cropping season. The green part of the leaves is stripped from the white midrib and prepared separately for freezing

Above: Purple sprouting broccoli is the hardiest of the broccolis and is excellent for freezing

Part 2
Vegetables

Globe Artichokes

Varieties. Grande Beurre and Green Globe are easily obtained varieties. Plants can be grown from seed but it is better to buy well-grown plants.

Cultivation. Soil should be in an open site, rich, well manured and deep.

Plant in April, rows 60 cm (2 ft) apart, 22 cm (9 in) between plants. Water well during the first season. Liquid feed from time to time. Protect plants with dry litter during winter, from November onwards, but uncover during long mild spells. In March mulch with a deep layer of well-rotted manure, home-made compost or seaweed compost.

Artichokes are best grown on a three-year rotation. In March or April scrape away the soil around established plants to expose shoots or suckers and reduce these to three a plant. Cut surplus away, each with a portion of root. Plant these in a row 10 cm (4 in) deep for a new crop. Repeat this practice each year, discarding three-year-old plants after they have cropped.

Harvesting. Cut flower heads when the bud is fully developed but before flower colour shows.

Jerusalem Artichokes

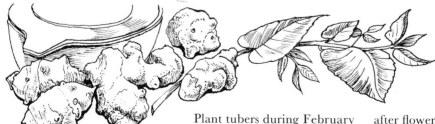

Varieties. The French variety Fuseau is recommended.

Cultivation. Choose a site with well-drained, rich but ordinary soil in a sunny position.

Plant tubers during February and onwards 45 cm (18 in) apart in rows 90 cm (3 ft) apart. Propagate by replanting saved tubers.

Plants remain better anchored if they are earthed up when 15 cm (6 in) high. Cut stems down after flowering, leaving a few centimetres of stalk to show where the tubers are.

Harvesting. Lift as required from November onwards. Tubers kept long out of the soil become shrivelled and dry.

Freezing

Preparation. Both types of artichoke freeze well and their delicious flavour is worth preserving. Globe artichokes must be frozen as soon as they are picked as they go stale quickly. Trim off the outer leaves and stalks, and wash the artichokes thoroughly. Remove the hairy 'chokes' from the centres. If you have a huge quantity of artichokes, the hearts alone may be frozen, in which case all the leaves and the 'choke' must first be removed. Jerusalem artichokes cannot be frozen whole, but should be peeled and cut in pieces, slightly softened in butter, then cooked in chicken stock and made into purée.

Blanching. Add 1 tablespoon lemon juice to 4·5 litres (8 pints) of water and blanch whole artichokes for 7 minutes. Blanch hearts for 5 minutes.

Packaging. Cool and drain upside down on absorbent paper. Pack in rigid containers, as polythene bags will tear. Pack hearts in polythene bags or rigid containers. Pack the purée in rigid containers, leaving a 1-cm (½ in) headspace.

Storage life. 12 months (globe artichokes), 3 months (Jerusalem artichoke purée).

Serving. Put whole frozen artichokes into boiling water, and boil for 10 minutes until the leaves are tender. Serve with melted butter, Hollandaise sauce or vinaigrette. Use hearts for cooked dishes. Reheat purée with more stock and milk to make soup.

Asparagus

Varieties. Recommended varieties include Connovers Colossal, Limburgia, Martha Washington and Brocks Imperial. Male plants crop better, so usually specially selected three-year-old plants bought from specialists are advised.

Cultivation. Soil should be deep, rich, light and preferably sandy, in an open, sunny site or with partial shade.

To raise plants from seed, sow in March three or four in a group 2 to 3 cm (1 in) deep, 35 to 40 cm (15 in) apart on a prepared bed. Thin later to one good plant to a station. Alternatively, sow on a nursery bed in 2 to 3-cm (1-in) deep drills, 30 cm (1 ft) apart. Thin out plants to 30 cm (1 ft) apart when 7 to 8 cm (3 in) high. Let plants remain until 2 to 3 years old, by which time it should be possible to cull the berry-producing female plants.

Any good raised bed can be used to grow asparagus. It does not have to be rectangular but the method of planting is important. Prepare the sites in advance so that as the roots are lifted or as soon as they arrive from the nursery they can be put into the ground.

The 'crowns' should be planted 45 cm (18 in) apart. Double rows should have 45 cm between them. Plant when the soil is warm, in late March or early April. There are two ways to plant. Traditionally, take out a trench the length of a row, 22 to 25 cm (9 to 10 in) deep and wide. Mark each plant station with a cane. Line the trench with well-rotted manure or home-made compost to a depth of 2 to 3 cm (1 in) or so. At the marked stations and around the canes pile it into heaps some 10 cm (4 in) high. Alternatively, use a good soil mixture of loam, peat, sand and balanced fertilizer, and if the soil is heavy, burnt earth. Take each crown and loosen the long, string-like roots so that you can sit the crown on top of the pile, and spread the roots down over it on all sides. Cover each plant as it is set in place; the roots should not be long exposed to the air.

Planting an asparagus crown. This should be set at the top of a small mound

Above: Green peppers, or capsicums, are grown in a manner similar to tomatoes, but they may need some protection if summer nights are cool

Right: Peppers can be frozen whole without blanching and kept for up to three months if just the seed and membranes are removed. Thaw at room temperature for one hour before stuffing

Sprinkle a little balanced fertilizer into the trench, or mix 2 parts superphosphate and 1 part sulphate of potash and apply this at a rate of 30 g (1 oz) per square metre or square yard. Fill in the trench and cover the plants to a depth of 10 to 12 cm (4 to 5 in). Firm the soil by treading it lightly.

The second method consists of making good planting holes at each station instead of making a trench.

Aftercare is important. Traditionally one should clean the bed each spring and sprinkle it with agricultural or even common salt at a rate of 25 to 30 g (1 oz) per square metre (square yard). This routine should be followed annually. However, if the bed contains other crops or is near to them, it might be advisable not to use salt. My own method is to wait until cutting is finished and then well fertilize the soil either with a good general fertilizer or by mixing together 5 parts superphosphate, 2 parts sulphate of potash and 1 part sulphate of ammonia and applying this at a rate of 250 g (9 oz) per square metre (square yard). In autumn cover the bed with a good mulch of well-rotted manure.

Harvesting. Begin cutting the shoots in the third year. They should be about 7 to 8 cm (3 in) above soil level. Take a sharp or special asparagus knife and thrust it diagonally into the soil at the side of the shoot so that you cut its stem some 10 cm (4 in) below the soil surface.

Freezing

Preparation. Asparagus must be frozen quickly after cutting, as it goes stale quickly. Wash the stems well, remove the woody ends and small scales. Cut the asparagus into 15-cm (6-in) lengths, and grade the stems according to thickness – small, medium and large. Do not tie the stems up into bundles.

Asparagus should be frozen quickly after cutting as it soon loses its freshness

Blanching. Each size should be blanched separately. Allow 2 minutes for small spears, 3 minutes for medium spears and 4 minutes for large spears. Cool and drain thoroughly.

Packaging. Pack in rigid containers, alternating the heads. Do not mix the sizes as it is then difficult to control the final cooking time. Seal, label and freeze.

Storage life. 9 months.

Serving. Put into boiling water and boil for 5 minutes. Serve with melted butter, Hollandaise sauce or vinaigrette. Frozen asparagus may also be used for a savoury flan or for making soup.

Broad beans

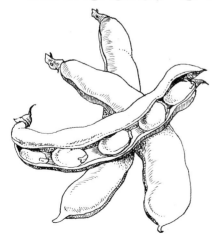

Varieties. Recommended varieties include Imperial White Windsor, Major, The Midget, Meteor, Express. The longpod varieties are the best for early crops. Other varieties do for maincrop. Dwarf varieties such as The Midget are excellent for small gardens. These crop well and produce small, sweet, tender beans.

Cultivation. Soil should be rich, well manured and moist on an open site for main crops and well drained, light and rich on a protected site or a south-facing border for early crops.

Broad beans can be sown from February to April in most gardens, but in cold areas it may be wise to delay sowing in the open until May. Cloches can be used to protect early sown rows. In very mild areas and in protected gardens broad beans may also be sown in the open in November to stand the winter and so crop the following year.

Seeds can be sown singly, dibbled individually into the soil

French beans

Varieties. Recommended varieties include Flair, Masterpiece, Sprite, Cordon, Romano (climbing).

There are both dwarf and climbing varieties of French or kidney beans. The advantage of the latter is that they mature earlier than runner beans.

Cultivation. Soil should be rich, well manured, non-acid, on an open, sunny site. Dust slightly acid soil with lime before sowing or planting.

Allow 14 weeks from sowing to the first picking. French beans do not need stringing or slicing, merely topping and tailing. For means of supporting climbing varieties see advice under Runner Beans.

French beans need a much higher temperature to germinate than do broad beans. The surest way to get good results is to start the seed off in warmth, that is, sown in pots or deep boxes under glass to be transplanted later. Alternatively, sow in the open ground and cover with cloches, guarding against mice and slugs. Warm the under-cloche soil first by incorporating plenty of humus into the drill. This method should also be followed later when making the first sowing in the open. Cover the strip to be sown in advance and when you see that the soil is in good condition,

7 to 8 cm (3 in) deep, 10 to 12 cm (4 to 5 in) apart and thinned out later to 22 to 23 cm (9 in) apart. Thinnings can be transplanted. Alternatively the seed can be sown in 7 to 8-cm (3-in) deep drills. Beans may also be sown in deep boxes or individually in small pots under glass, hardened off when growing well and planted out in mid-April or thereabouts according to weather.

Space is saved if broad beans are sown in double rows, with 15 cm (6 in) between the two rows. If several double rows are grown, allow 60 cm (2 ft) between them. Dwarf broad beans are bushier in habit and single rows will suffice.

Harvesting. Allow 18 weeks from sowing time to first picking. When the first flowers appear, nip out the tips of the plants (these 'greens' can be eaten) to encourage growth of bean pods and to discourage colonization by blackfly.

Sowing a double row of broad beans

Freezing

Preparation. Use only small young broad beans with tender skins. Remove from the pods and discard any blemished beans.

Blanching. Blanch for $1\frac{1}{2}$ minutes.

Packaging. Open freeze and pack in polythene bags. Seal and label.

Storage life. 12 months.

Serving. Put into boiling salted water and cook for 8 minutes. Serve with butter and a little crisply cooked chopped bacon, or with parsley sauce. Cold broad beans make a good salad with oil and vinegar dressing.

Left: Winter cauliflowers mature from January to May. They like a rich, moisture-retentive soil

Above: Cauliflower makes an appetizing supper dish when served with a cheese sauce and, as shown here, with crisply grilled bacon rolls

French beans are delicious served with butter and, if liked, with the addition of a little grated onion

remove the cloches, sow and re-cover. In this way French beans can be sown as early as mid-March in the South and a week or two later in the North, depending on the season. Usually, though, it is prudent to delay sowing until late April. If seeds germinate quickly, they will grow and mature quickly also.

The best seasons for sowing seed in the open are at the end of April (delay if the weather is cool and wet), the middle of May, the beginning of June and the end of July. Usually late-sown seed germinates very well because of the high soil temperature. Should the season be dry, water the drill well before sowing. Late sowings

will need to be covered by cloches once the cold nights begin.

Only three out of four beans germinate, so allow for this when sowing. In the open sow them 7 to 8 cm (3 in) apart, 5 cm (2 in) deep in drills and later remove surplus plants to give 15-cm (6-in) intervals between each. Thinnings can be transplanted when the soil is moist or after watering and will mature at a slightly different rate.

Encourage the plants to grow by watering them during dry periods. Feed them with a liquid manure when the pods form to help keep the plants in bloom and cropping well.

Harvesting. Pick the pods while the beans inside are still small and immature.

Freezing

Preparation. Use only young tender beans, about the thickness of a bootlace. Remove tops and tails from the beans, and if necessary any strings. Freeze the small ones whole, or cut into 2·5-cm (1-in) pieces.

Blanching. Blanch whole beans for 3 minutes and cut beans for 2 minutes.

Packaging. Cool, drain and pack in polythene bags. Seal and label.

Storage life. 12 months.

Serving. Put into boiling water and cook whole beans for 7 minutes, cut beans for 5 minutes. Toss in a little butter, with the addition of a little grated onion if liked.

Runner beans

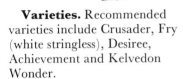

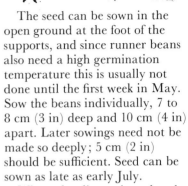

Varieties. Recommended varieties include Crusader, Fry (white stringless), Desiree, Achievement and Kelvedon Wonder.

Cultivation. Soil should be light but rich, well manured and non-acid, on a sunny or only partially shaded site. In hot weather runner beans must be watered, so it is advisable to have this fact in mind when planning the site. Beans can be grown on the same ground year after year.

Although there are dwarf varieties of runner beans and although even the climbing varieties can be kept dwarf and bushy by nipping out the tips of the shoots, these are not as satisfactory as those which are encouraged to climb. Runner beans are quite decorative and can be grown over archways above a path to save space, up trelliswork to act as screens or as arbours. It is possible to buy special netting to support beans and they can also be grown up a wire netting screen, on the walls of a fruit cage for example.

Traditionally they are grown in a double row, a plant to each pole or two plants sharing a pole. These poles, which are driven into the ground, are sloped towards the centre of the two rows and lashed to a horizontal crossbar some feet from the ground. This form of support should be made really strong because a double row of beans in full crop can be very heavy. A simpler method and one which is becoming popular commercially as well as among home gardeners is to make a tripod or group of tall, strong canes. These also are pushed into the ground, sloped and then lashed together at the top, wigwam-like, with a plant set at the foot of each cane. These groups are very neat and easy to erect.

Since beans are usually grown on the same site year after year, it follows that it is good practice to prepare the site during winter so that the soil shall be good and retentive of moisture when the crop is planted. Traditionally a trench is dug in winter along the site where the row is to be made. The base of the trench should be forked to encourage a deep root run. Ideally, when filled, the trench should contain 7 to 8 cm (3 in) of good manure or home-made compost topped with twice this depth of good soil. It is worth time and trouble mixing this. Alternatively, instead of preparing a trench, always keep the soil well mulched. Plants in pod always respond to a little liquid feeding and any shortcomings in the richness of the soil can usually be adjusted at this time.

The seed can be sown in the open ground at the foot of the supports, and since runner beans also need a high germination temperature this is usually not done until the first week in May. Sow the beans individually, 7 to 8 cm (3 in) deep and 10 cm (4 in) apart. Later sowings need not be made so deeply; 5 cm (2 in) should be sufficient. Seed can be sown as late as early July.

Where the climate is cool and where slugs or other pests are present, the seed can be sown in pots or deep boxes from the end of April to early May. It is best to use small individual pots or other containers for each seed so that the young plants suffer little or no check on transplanting. Plant them outdoors during the first week in June or onwards, 20 cm (8 in) between each plant.

Harvesting. Pick the pods while young, before they become tough and stringy. They should be no longer than 18 cm (7 in).

Freezing

Preparation. Do not shred the beans finely, but string and slice them thickly in chunks.

Blanching. Blanch for 2 minutes.

Packaging. Cool, drain and pack them in polythene bags. Seal and label.

Storage life. 12 months.

Serving. Put into boiling water and cook for 7 minutes. Season well with salt and pepper and toss in butter.

Above: Young, even-sized leeks are the best for freezing. It is important that they should be washed thoroughly in cold, running water

Right: Marrows like a rich, warm soil with plenty of humus. When intended for freezing they should be gathered young while still very small

Beet

It is important for new gardeners to appreciate that the beet family contains kinds other than those grown for their roots. There are also leaf beets, more widely known perhaps by such names as Perpetual spinach, Spinach beet, Swiss chard and Seakale beet according to the variety.

Beetroot

Varieties. Recommended varieties include Bolthardy, Suttons Globe, Detroit Little Ball, Burpee's Golden. Cheltenham Green Top, with long roots, has greener foliage than the other varieties. It is a good kind to grow where both tops and roots are wanted.

Cultivation. Soil should be light, sandy for preference, otherwise well charged with humus and peat.

Although beetroots are grown mainly for their roots, their leaves, like those of the leaf beets, are edible and delicious. They can be cooked on their own, when they lose much of their red colouring, or they can be mixed with other leaf beets or lettuce. They also freeze well.

Root beets vary according to their variety or kind, being round, cylindrical and long or parsnip-shaped. They are also deep crimson, yellow or white, the last two varieties being non-staining.

Although mature beetroots store well, full value is often not gained from this crop. When the roots are lifted in October or November the leaves need not be thrown away. They can be saved and frozen as spinach.

Globe and cylindrical varieties are most delicious when eaten young, even very young. This means that the plants need not occupy garden space for a very long period, a good point where the garden is small.

The soil for beets should be rich so that the roots will grow quickly, but it should not be freshly manured because this tends to

Beetroot for freezing should be pulled while still small and young

make the roots misshapen or forked. The best crops are raised on land which has been liberally manured for the previous crop grown on it.

The seed of globe varieties can be sown outdoors in April if the soil is warm or if it has been warmed under cloches, or at any time from then until July. Roots should be ready to pull in about 16 weeks. Seed can be sown in March if the crop is to be grown in frames or under cloches and kept covered until the frosts are finished. Beet to be lifted for storing should be sown from mid-May to early June. Thin seedlings of storage beet so that they are 15 cm (6 in) apart.

The round, rough-surfaced seeds, large enough to handle individually, are in fact capsules, which means that seedlings appear in clusters. Space the seed along shallow drills about 5 cm (2 in) apart. Make rows 30 to 40 cm (12 to 15 in) apart. To get full value from a row, let the seedlings grow to 5 to 8 cm (2 to 3 in) high and make the first thinning so that the plants are about 5 cm (2 in) apart, leaving the largest seedling in each case.

Harvesting. The thinnings can be cooked or eaten raw in salads. Later, when the roots are just touching, pull again taking alternate roots which by then should be large enough to eat. Continue pulling small alternate roots each time until the remaining roots are large enough to clear completely.

Freezing

Preparation. Only use small young beetroot no more than 7·5 cm (3 in) in diameter. Blanching makes them tough and rubbery when frozen, so they must be cooked completely. Wash the beetroot and trim the leaves, but not too close to the beetroot or they will 'bleed' during cooking. Sort the beetroot into sizes and start cooking the larger ones first, then add the small ones at 10-minute intervals according to size, so they all finish cooking together. Cool quickly in running water and rub off the skins.

Packaging. If the beetroot are under 2·5 cm (1 in) in diameter, they may be packed whole. Slice or dice the larger ones. Pack in polythene bags or rigid containers. Seal and label.

Storage life. 6 months.

Serving. Thaw the beetroot in the container for about 3 hours in the refrigerator. Drain them and serve with vinegar, or a sour cream dressing.

Leaf beet

Varieties. Recommended varieties include Perpetual Spinach, Swiss Chard, Burpee Golden Beet Leaves.

Cultivation. Perpetual spinach or spinach beet is so named because it has a very long season. Seed can be sown in spring for summer use and in the autumn for winter and spring, although in fact the one spring sowing will often suffice and the plants will carry on until it is time to sow the following year's crop, when they should be dug up and discarded. The same is true of the thick, white-ribbed Swiss Chard (or seakale beet). The plants are

When harvesting leaf beet, a few outer leaves should be cut from each plant

Below: When sweet corn cobs are ready for harvesting the kernels will be found to contain a milky fluid. They can be frozen whole, or the kernels can be scraped off after blanching and packed in rigid containers

Right: To encourage the fruit to mature, the growing tip of outdoor tomatoes should be pinched out when four trusses of fruit have formed

hardy but the crop is improved if they are cloche-covered in winter.

Leaf beets should be grown under the same conditions as beetroots, but as the individual plants grow so much larger, especially the Swiss Chard, thin to 22 cm (9 in) apart, rows 45 cm (18 in) apart.

Harvesting. Swiss Chard is a very economical crop since the outer green can be stripped from the white midribs and both can be cooked separately.

To gather leaf beets, take one or two outer leaves from each plant in the row, cutting them with a knife.

Freezing

Preparation. The leaves have to be separated for freezing. Strip the glossy leaves from the midribs and prepare separately.

Blanching. Blanch the green

leaves for 2 minutes. Cut the midribs into 5-cm (2-in) sticks and blanch for 3 minutes.

Packaging. Cool and drain both the leaves and midribs and pack separately in polythene bags.

Storage life. 12 months.

Serving. Cook the green leaves for 7 minutes in a little butter or dripping, without any water. Cook the midribs in boiling water for 7 minutes, drain and toss in butter.

Broccoli

Varieties. Winter cauliflower, often called broccoli, is described in the section on Cauliflower.

Recommended varieties include Calabrese, Suttons Express Corona, Green Sprouting, Italian Sprouting, Autumn Spear.

The kind of sprouting broccoli you grow should depend mainly on the situation of the garden. Of them all, the purple sprouting varieties are the hardiest. The white sprouting, really green, is susceptible to frost. Both this and the purple are ready to pick in early winter and spring according to the variety. On the other hand, the green calabrese is ready from August, through September until late autumn, again according to variety. This type therefore is particularly useful to those who garden in cold areas. A late summer crop could provide plenty of succulent broccoli to freeze for winter supplies. This broccoli is slightly different in appearance and habit from the other kinds.

Cultivation. The soil should not be greatly enriched and ideally they should follow a root crop.

Allow plenty of space for broccoli, at least 75 cm (2½ ft) each way. Use the nursery bed system

Picking the flowering shoots of purple sprouting broccoli

for all but the autumn cropping varieties. Sow the former in April and May and try to have them in their final places by late June or July. The calabrese varieties need to get off to an early start. Sow these in February in boxes of light soil at about 17°C (65°F). As soon as the true leaves are sturdy, transplant the seedlings under a cloche or in a frame so that they gradually become hardened. Plant them in the open ground in June, 60 to 75 cm (2 to 2½ ft) apart each way.

If broccoli are allowed to grow lush they will succumb to frost. Plant them firmly. Use a trowel for planting and afterwards press down on each side of the plant with the foot so that it is well and truly anchored.

Harvesting. When broccoli is ready a few large shoots are produced on each plant. These can be snapped off or cut to the required length. This picking induces smaller shoots to appear from the base of the cut stem. Successive shoots become smaller and smaller until it is often more economic to pull up the plant and use the space it occupies for a new crop.

Calabrese, on the other hand, first produces a large central shoot or head, which may be cooked whole or divided. When this is cut, other much smaller though still useful shoots are produced from the base of the leaves growing around it. These are long stemmed and are usually cut at about 15 cm (6 in), although if the plant is well grown the whole stem length should be succulent and useful.

In average years the sequence is as follows: Early Purple Sprouting, Jan. and Feb.; Purple Sprouting, March; Late Purple Sprouting, April; Early White Sprouting, Feb.; Late White, April. If you grow more than one of these their seasons will overlap because most broccoli plants are productive for two or three months according to the variety.

Freezing

Preparation. Use compact heads of uniform colour with tender stalks not more than 2·5 cm (1 in) thick. Trim off the woody stems and outer leaves. Wash very thoroughly in salted water, 2 teaspoons salt to 4 to 5 litres (8 pints) water, for 30 minutes, and rinse in clean, cold water.

Blanching. Blanch for 3 minutes (thin stems), 4 minutes (medium stems), 5 minutes (thick stems).

Packaging. Cool and drain, and pack in rigid containers, alternating the heads, to avoid crushing and bruising. Seal and label.

Storage life. 12 months.

Serving. Put into boiling water and cook for 8 minutes. Drain well and serve with butter or Hollandaise sauce. Broccoli and calabrese are also delicious served slightly warm in an oil and vinegar dressing.

Right: Packing blanched sprigs of broccoli alternately head to tail in foil containers

Top: The green calabrese first produces a large central shoot which may be cooked whole or divided. Smaller shoots are produced from the base of the leaves

Above: Fully cooked dishes freeze well and are useful time savers. These stuffed courgettes are being packed in foil containers for freezing

Right: Asparagus is delicious served with melted butter or used as a filling for a flan or savoury pancake

Brussels sprouts

Varieties. Recommended varieties include: Peer Gynt, Prince Askold, Roodneff, Early Button, Siltex, Fasolt.

Cultivation. Soil should be good, rich, well manured and limed, reasonably heavy (sprouts do not do well on light soils), firm, on almost any site except one which is very exposed.

Early varieties which produce sprouts in autumn (ideal for those with cold winter gardens) should be sown in boxes placed in frames or under cloches in early January until early February. It is important to get an early start.

Sprouts to be picked in winter should be sown in a nursery bed or in the row where they are to mature, in which case they should be thinned out from mid-March to mid-April. These should be in their final stations, 60 cm (2 ft) each way in May or June. Varieties which produce large sprouts need 75 cm (2½ ft) between plants. Brussels sprouts seem to do best if they are set in their final places while the plants are still quite small.

As with broccoli, it is important to firm the plants after they are put in the soil. Unless this is firm they will not make tight buttons. In windy gardens it is beneficial to stake the plants. This prevents them from moving around and enlarging the stem holes at ground level.

Harvesting. Sprout rows can be profitably cleared in spring. When the remaining sprouts are seen to become elongated, the tops can be cut and used as spring greens.

Freezing

Preparation. Use small compact sprouts, clean them and remove any discoloured leaves. Grade for size.

Blanching. Blanch 3 minutes (small), 4 minutes (medium), and avoid over-blanching which results in soggy, discoloured sprouts which smell unpleasant. Put a teaspoon of vinegar in the blanching water to avoid a smell.

Packaging. Cool and drain. Open freeze and pack in polythene bags. Seal and label.

Storage life. 12 months.

Serving. Put into boiling water and cook for 8 minutes. Serve with butter, or a little grated cheese. Sprouts can be combined with cooked chestnuts, onions or celery.

Red cabbage

Varieties. Recommended varieties include: Ruby Ball, Large Blood Red, Niggy Novelty.

Cultivation. Soil should be ordinary, good, rich, firm and slightly alkaline.

Since this is the basis of so many good dishes, red cabbage is well worth growing. It can be raised in a seed bed just like any of the other brassicas which have been described. The thing to bear in mind is that it needs a longer maturing period than the green cabbages.

For autumn or late summer use, sow the seed in March. For winter sow in late April or early May, and since these cabbages

Red cabbage can be frozen either shredded and blanched or fully cooked

44

are tender, protect with cloches later. If you like really large firm heads, sow the seed in August and either cover the pricked-off seedlings with a cloche or put them in a frame. Plant them out in March or April. Keep the plants growing well, so water them during any dry spells.

Harvesting. Ready for use in late summer and autumn.

Freezing

Preparation. Red cabbage may be prepared in two ways for freezing. It can be shredded and blanched, or fully cooked, which gives better results. To freeze cooked, shred the cabbage and then add 15 g ($\frac{1}{2}$ oz) butter, 1 medium chopped onion, 1 tablespoon brown sugar, 1 tablespoon cider vinegar, salt and pepper, 150 ml ($\frac{1}{4}$ pint) dry cider and 2 chopped small tart apples to each 1 kg (2 lb) cabbage. Cover and simmer for 1 hour.

Blanching. Blanch shredded cabbage for 1$\frac{1}{2}$ minutes.

Packaging. To freeze blanched cabbage, pack in polythene bags, seal and label. Pack cooked cabbage in a rigid container.

Storage life. 12 months (blanched cabbage), 2 months (cooked cabbage).

Serving. Cook blanched cabbage in boiling water for 8 minutes. Reheat cooked cabbage in a casserole in a moderate oven (180°C, 350°F, Gas Mark 4) for 1 hour, and serve with pork, bacon, or hotpot.

Capsicum

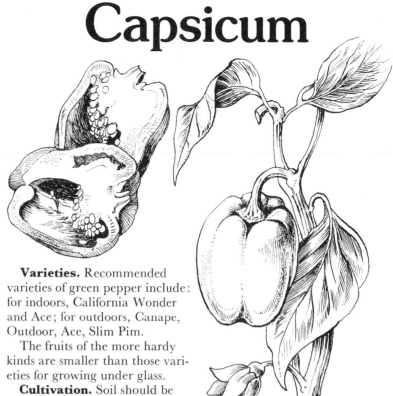

Varieties. Recommended varieties of green pepper include: for indoors, California Wonder and Ace; for outdoors, Canape, Outdoor, Ace, Slim Pim.

The fruits of the more hardy kinds are smaller than those varieties for growing under glass.

Cultivation. Soil should be light but rich, with plenty of humus and moisture retentive. It helps to have a sunny site, preferably against a south-facing wall.

The method for growing capsicums or peppers is very much the same as that for tomatoes, so follow details given in that section. However, there are a few special points about capsicums. If they are to be grown outdoors be sure to select a variety which will mature quickly in our cooler climate.

Should the nights be cool in summer, protect the entire plant by pulling a large plastic bag over it. Remove this before the sun reaches the plant next morning.

Germination and early growth are both slow, so be patient. Sow seeds individually into small pots in a temperature of at least 18°C (68°F).

Harvesting. Green peppers can be cut when they are large enough. They will turn red or yellow, according to variety, if left to ripen.

Freezing

Preparation. Use plump, firm peppers with glossy skins. Wash and wipe them, cut off the stems and remove the seeds and membranes. Freeze as halves, slices, dice or rings. Whole peppers for stuffing may be frozen without blanching, with only the stem, seeds and membranes removed.

Blanching. Blanch 3 minutes (halves) or 2 minutes (slices, dice or rings).

Packaging. Cool and drain and pack in polythene bags. Seal and label. Pack unblanched whole peppers in polythene bags, seal and label carefully with date.

Storage life. 12 months (blanched), 3 months (unblanched).

Serving. Slices, dice and rings may be put into dishes while still frozen. To use half or whole peppers for cooking, thaw for 1 hour at room temperature before stuffing.

Above: Raspberries which have been open frozen can be packed dry in polythene bags or firm containers

Right: Shredded red cabbage can be open frozen and packed in a rigid container, but it also freezes well if it is fully cooked

Carrots

Varieties. There are different kinds of carrots. Shorthorn, as the name implies, are like a short, conical horn. Stump-rooted varieties are of medium length and blunt at the end. Intermediate are finger-shaped and neither short nor long. Long-rooted have the classic long, tapering shape.

Recommended varieties include: Amstel, Amsterdam Forcing Sweetheart, Chantenay Red Cored, Nantes Kurna and Pioneer.

Cultivation. Best soil is deep, with plenty of humus, manured for a previous crop or in a previous year, a sandy loam with a high water table.

It is important that carrots grow quickly, especially if you wish to pull tender baby roots. The more open the soil texture and the lighter and easier it is to work, the better the carrots will be. Land too recently manured, or one in which there is too much nitrogenous fertilizer, will tend to make the roots fork, to split and become fibrous.

You can begin sowing shorthorn carrot seed as early as February if you can find a well-sheltered place, perhaps among other crops under cloches, or in a warm, raised border. Quick-maturing early varieties can also be sown in March and April in the open ground. They should be ready to pull in June and on through July. They can also be sown in succession up to mid-July. Sow the next row when the previous one appears above the soil. Intermediate varieties take about three months to mature, but you can pull some of these while they are quite young and thin the rows at the same time.

Maincrop carrots can be sown as late as May and June, or perhaps to follow some other crop which is finished early, in July. These should be encouraged to grow quickly. Apply plenty of water so that by autumn they have made large roots.

If you have cloches to spare you can sow an early variety in August in the North and September or October elsewhere to pull young for Christmas.

You can sow carrot seed broadcast, a good method to use if you have a warm border somewhere, perhaps at the foot of a fruit tree growing against a wall, or on a piece of land the width of a cloche.

In rows, sow in shallow drills, with rows 22 cm (9 in) apart. Sow thinly and thin out as soon as you can handle the seedlings. Thin at first to just 2 to 3 cm (1 in) apart and let the remaining roots swell. Then take out alternate plants until the space between them is about 10 cm (4 in) for store crops and a little less for baby carrots. You can judge the size you want as you pull them.

Harvesting. Only early small young carrots are worth freezing.

Freezing

Preparation. Remove the tops, wash and scrape well. Leave very small ones whole, but slice or dice larger ones.

Blanching. Blanch 3 minutes (whole) or 2 minutes (sliced or diced).

Packaging. Cool, drain and pack in polythene bags. Seal and label.

Storage life. 12 months.

Serving. Put into boiling water and cook for 8 minutes.

Cauliflower

Varieties. Almost all varieties of cauliflower freeze well, so it becomes mainly a question of which variety is most convenient for you to grow.

Recommended varieties include: for summer and autumn, Snowball, All the Year Round, August Crop, Canberra and Dominant. For winter, Armado May, Mirado, St George, Veitch's Self Protecting, Leamington.

Cultivation. Soil should be rich but not newly manured, retentive of moisture, well limed, on a sheltered site for winter varieties which, incidentally, are good subjects for gardens in the north of the country.

For small gardens the new Australian varieties are dwarf growing. If these are sown outdoors in late April or May, they can be harvested from September onwards, depending on variety.

Winter cauliflowers mature in January and onwards until May. These also are sown in late April and May. Autumn varieties complete the cycle. These also are sown in spring.

Use the nursery bed method and put the seedlings out while they are still quite young from 45 cm (18 in) to 90 cm (3 ft) apart. See that they are kept well watered, otherwise they will not grow but will remain static and make only tiny, button-sized heads.

A word of explanation. 'Self-protecting' means that the leaves protect the white curd at the heart. Those which do not protect themselves tend to become discoloured by frost. For this reason it is wise to snap the midrib of some of the outer leaves so that they bend and cover the curds. Once the head is cut the plant is of no further value and should be lifted.

Harvesting. A freezer has made it much more profitable to produce cauliflowers in the average garden simply because these are vegetables which tend to come into production all at once, or at least with only a few days between some and the rest. With a freezer all can be gathered when they are at their peak.

Freezing

Preparation. Cauliflowers may be frozen in sprigs, but if the heads are small, they may be frozen whole. Use firm heads with close white 'curds'. Wash very thoroughly and break into sprigs.

Blanching. Add the juice of 1 lemon to the blanching water, and blanch for 3 minutes.

Packaging. Cool and drain and pack in polythene bags. Seal and label. Sprigs can also be open frozen.

Bending over the leaves of a cauliflower to protect the curd from frost damage

Storage life. 6 months.

Serving. Put the sprigs into boiling water and cook for 10 minutes; 15 minutes for whole heads. Cauliflower should be served slightly crisp. Toss in butter and seasoning, or serve with a white or cheese sauce.

Open freezing blanched cauliflower sprigs. These are then packed in polythene bags

Above: If there is sufficient space, blackberries can be allowed to grow naturally, or they can be trained on wires for easy picking

Right: A tray of open-frozen blackberries. These can now be packed and stored in polythene bags without sticking together

Celery

Varieties. There are two types of celery, summer and winter. Summer celery can be 'white' (really pale yellow), so-called 'self-blanching' or the American green variety. Summer celery is easier to grow but it has not such a long season.

Recommended varieties include: American Green, Golden Self-Blanching, Prizetaker, Giant Pink, Giant Red, New Dwarf White.

Cultivation. Soil should be rich and moisture retentive, so apply plenty of humus, well-rotted compost, manure, mushroom compost, leafmould or peat. It should be well limed before planting.

Sow the seed for all varieties as finely as possible in boxes of light soil. Just cover the seed. Celery is sometimes slow to germinate. If you want an early crop of winter celery, sow the first batch of seed in February at about 18 to 22°C (65 to 75°F). Sow in early March for the other winter kinds. Sow in late March for the summer kinds. Prick out the seedlings into boxes 5 cm (2 in) apart as soon as they are large enough to handle, but begin hardening them off in late April. Plant out in June. Alternatively, plant them 15 cm (6 in) apart in some sheltered, outdoor, shady bed until you are ready to put them in their trenches. It is important not to allow them to become starved in their boxes.

Summer celery

Although summer celery does not have to be earthed up as does the winter kind, it is still important that as much light as possible should be kept from the stems of the self-blanching varieties. The American green varieties appear to need no earthing up or blanching.

Cultivation. Plants should be set in blocks and not in rows so that they help to blanch each other. A frame is considered to be the best method and it is easy to fix boards, hardboard or plastic around the plants. A 2-m by 1-m (6-ft by 4-ft) frame should hold 24 or so plants, set 22 cm (9 in) apart. If no frame is available, the plants can be surrounded with boards or with black plastic sheeting.

Water the plants well during dry seasons and liberally from July onwards so that the stems are really succulent. Feed them frequently also with a weak liquid fertilizer. Watch for slugs.

Harvesting. Once they are ready the plants tend to bolt, which means that if they are not cut then, instead of a nice heart of overlapping succulent stems, a thick, tough, elongated central stem is produced. Fortunately the heads can be cooked and frozen and so contribute to the winter store of vegetables.

Take from the outer row of the block first and move the boards or whatever is used close to the next row of plants every time a gap is made.

Winter celery

This can be white, pink and red. The red variety is the hardiest and so is best for cold areas, or it can be grown to follow one of the less hardy varieties. It has a fine flavour. The pink is better flavoured than the white.

Cultivation. Ideally 30-cm (1-ft) deep trenches should be prepared to accommodate the plants, so that they can be flooded from time to time. Trenches are spaced about 1 m (3 ft) apart when more than one row is grown, but the ridged soil between them can be used for quick-growing summer crops such as radish, lettuce and spinach. The trenches should be 35 to 40 cm (15 in) wide for a single row of plants, 45 cm (18 in) for double. Naturally, the soil in the trench should be rich. It should contain a deep layer of well-rotted animal manure which is best forked into the floor of the trench some weeks before planting.

The young plants should go into their places by the beginning of June for early crops and at the end of June or in July for the main crop, 20 cm (8 in) apart with 15 cm (6 in) between the double rows. After planting the trench should be flooded.

If instead of trenches you make deep drills, you should be able to grow quite good celery. The thing to bear in mind is that the

Planting out celery in a trench which has been well manured some weeks before

plants should never become dry at the roots. In dry spells flood trenches and deep drills, even if you can spare nothing more than water from the weekly wash.

Liquid feeding is also important. This is best given after watering. Apart from this, apply superphosphate, a good celery fertilizer, at a rate of 30 g (1 oz) to 2 m (6 ft) of row, no more, one month after planting and again a month later.

When the plants are about 30 cm (1 ft) tall and the stems well formed, begin blanching in August or September. Tie the stems together so that they are cupped neatly, keeping soil out of the heart as you do this. Remove side shoots or low-growing leaves, saving them for flavouring. Gradually, in fine weather, draw the soil from the sides of the trench around the stems until finally it is right up to the leaves.

Other means of blanching can be employed, useful for plants not grown in deep trenches. Celery collars are on sale at garden centres and shops, or

Tying paper collars round celery to keep the heart clean while earthing up

drain pipes or black plastic tubes are sometimes slipped over the plants. Even brown paper is used. Beware, though, of slugs, which can get inside and will greatly damage if not destroy the celery heart.

Harvesting. If the garden or the weather is very cold during winter, use a cloche over part of the row so that some plants are

ready to lift when required. If you can get bracken, protect rows with a cover of this in severe weather. Lift the entire root with a fork.

Freezing

Preparation. Celery loses its crispness when frozen and cannot be used without further cooking. Use tender crisp stalks and remove any strings. Wash very well and cut into 2·5 cm (1 in) lengths.

Blanching. Blanch for 3 minutes.

Packaging. Cool and drain, and pack dry in polythene bags. Seal and label. If preferred, pack in some of the blanching liquid in rigid containers, leaving a 1-cm ($\frac{1}{2}$-in) headspace.

Storage life. 12 months.

Serving. Cook dry celery pieces in water, milk or stock until tender. Celery pieces in liquid can be added, while still frozen, to soups and stews.

Courgettes and marrows

Varieties. Recommended varieties include: Zuccini F_1 Hybrid, Aristocrat, True French.

Cultivation. Soil should be ordinary but good, rich with plenty of humus, warm and on a sunny or only partially shaded site.

Courgettes and marrows are raised in the same way. The seeds can be sown directly in the soil or plants can be raised individually in pots.

For the first method prepare the stations by making sure that the soil is good (see page 11). Allow about 1 square metre (1 square yard) for each plant. In May sow two or three seeds at

each place in case one alone should not germinate. Water the soil and cover with a cloche. Later thin the seedlings to one at each place. The thinnings can be transplanted. Leave the plants covered until June but make sure that they do not dry out.

For the second method sow the seeds singly, on edge, in pots of moist soil in a heated frame, in a greenhouse or on a sunny windowsill. Repot the seedlings as soon as the roots have filled the first pot so that growth is not checked.

If cloches are available, courgettes can be planted out of doors at the end of April. Failing this, begin hardening them off in May, standing the pots outdoors by day. Plant them out during the first week in June. Water them well so that they grow fast and use weak liquid manures.

Harvesting. The marrow family produces many delicious and easily grown vegetables besides marrows themselves, squash of many varieties and pumpkins. Most of these can be

Above: Though apples cannot be frozen whole to eat raw, they are excellent for cooking. They can be sliced and packed in sugar or syrup, or cooked and puréed before freezing

Right: Gooseberries may·be grown as bushes, but the cordon forms take less room and are easier for picking

Slicing courgettes ready for blanching or tossing in butter before freezing

Freezing

Preparation. Use tender young courgettes or very small marrows. Do not peel, but wipe with a damp cloth and cut into 1-cm ($\frac{1}{2}$-in) slices. Older marrows keep well in a dry place, but they may be cooked and made into purée for freezing.

Blanching. Blanch for 1 minute. Alternatively, toss slices in butter until just tender.

Packaging. Open freeze water-blanched slices, pack in polythene bags, seal and label. Pack fried slices in small quantities in rigid containers or polythene bags. Pack marrow purée in rigid containers, leaving a 1-cm ($\frac{1}{2}$-in) headspace.

Storage life. 12 months (water-blanched); 3 months (fried slices or purée).

Serving. Fry water-blanched or fried slices in hot oil and season well. Reheat marrow purée in a double saucepan and add butter and seasoning.

left on the plant to swell and ripen thoroughly, after which they can be stored and will keep for many months. Courgettes, however, should be gathered quite young, as soon as the little bloom on the end of the fruit fades and is ready to drop off. Left to grow larger than this, they become marrows. When intended for freezing marrows, too, should be gathered while young and still very small.

Courgette varieties are specially bred to crop prolifically, which means that it is often possible to gather some each day from well-grown plants, usually far too many for immediate consumption. This being the case it is obviously profitable to freeze the surplus.

Leeks

Varieties. Recommended varieties include: The Lyon, Prizetaker, Marble Pillar, Abel.

Cultivation. Soil should be deep, well manured, porous and easy to work, on an open, sunny site.

Leeks pay for attention, but it is possible to grow them with little trouble, for instance sowing the seed thinly in March where the plants are to mature, in shallow drills 30 cm (1 ft) apart. Later the seedlings should be thinned to 5 to 8 cm (2 to 3 in) apart. The thinnings can be transplanted. To blanch the stem the soil should be earthed up gradually on each side of the plants to keep out the light.

The other and better method is to sow the seed on a seed bed in a row in the open ground, or in heat in boxes. From nursery rows and boxes the seedlings should be transplanted as soon as they can be handled, either to deeper boxes or individual pots, or simply to give each plant more space in the nursery bed.

They can be planted in the open ground in summer. Planting is done in a special way. Use a garden line and make holes beside it with a pointed dibber, each to a depth of 15 cm (6 in) or so. As each hole is made, drop a plant into it. You should just see the tips of its leaves above the soil level.

I like to dribble in a little peat and then a little water into the hole. See that the plant remains upright and visible. The holes will gradually fill up and the stem below the soil will become blanched. You can make an even greater length of blanched stem if you make the holes at the bottom of a drill, but to do this it follows that the soil must be very deep and easily worked.

Otherwise, to make a greater portion of blanched stem, earth up the plants as you do potatoes, when the soil is in good condition during late summer and autumn.

Harvesting. Take a long fork to lift the leeks when they are required. Use them by the spring or they will go to seed.

Freezing

Preparation. Use young even-sized leeks. Remove the coarse outer leaves and trim off the green tops. Wash very thoroughly indeed in cold running water. Cut larger leeks into 1-cm ($\frac{1}{2}$-in) rings.

Blanching. Blanch 2 minutes (slices), 3 minutes (whole).

Packaging. Cool and drain very thoroughly, and pack in small quantities in polythene bags or rigid containers. Overwrap the bags as leeks smell strongly. Seal and label.

Storage life. 6 months.

Serving. Add, while still frozen, to soups or stews, or toss in a little butter before adding. To serve as a vegetable, cook the frozen sliced leeks in a covered heavy saucepan or in a moderate oven (180°C, 350°F, Gas Mark 4) in a casserole, with a knob of butter, salt and pepper, for 20 minutes. Leeks may also be served in white sauce, and are good cooked and added to a hot potato salad, or an omelette.

Planting leeks. Deep, straight holes are made with a pointed dibber

Peas

Varieties. There are probably more peas deep frozen than any other vegetable, both commercially and at home. This means that a considerable amount of research has been carried out to determine the best varieties for this purpose. Fortunately there are some in each of the three groups into which these vegetables are divided. These are Earlies, ready for picking after 12 weeks; Second Earlies, ready after 13 to 14 weeks and Maincrop, ready after 14 to 15 weeks. To these we should add the delectable Mange-tout or Sugar Peas, which can be treated as Earlies and then sown in succession like Maincrop if required.

Recommended varieties include Earlies: Hurst's Beagle, Early Onward, Kelvedon Wonder, Vitalis, Petit Pois Gullivert. Second Earlies and Maincrop: Recette, Victory Freezer, Petit Pois Gullivert, Chieftain, Achievement, Greenshaft. Mange-tout: Sugar Dwarf Sweetgreen, Oregon Sugar Pod, Dwarf de Grace.

Cultivation. Soil should be slightly acid but deep and rich in humus, moisture retentive, on an open, sunny site, protected for those varieties sown in late autumn and early spring.

All can be sown at about the same time, in March or April, according to weather conditions. Where succession is required, as a general rule sow again when the seeds sown previously show above the soil. It is possible by sowing early and using cloches in a warm and protected site, to pick peas in May. Those whose aim is to produce plenty of peas for freezing might be best advised to concentrate on the later and usually heavier crops which are less demanding.

The First Earlies usually hit the best weather for peas. Later varieties sometimes have to struggle to grow under drought conditions, but on the other hand many Maincrops have a superb flavour. Much depends on whether or not it is possible to water the crops in a dry spell.

Peas are usually sown in double or even treble rows with 7 to 8 cm (3 in) between the seeds each way. Drills should be 7 cm (3 in) deep. When you grow more than one row of peas, keep the distance between them roughly the same as the height of the plants, that is about 1 m (1 yd) high, 1 m (1 yd) between the rows. Guard against mice, birds and slugs in the early stages, and again against birds when the peas are swelling in the pods. Once the seedlings are through the soil the supports should be put in place.

Most peas, even the so-called dwarf varieties, crop best when supported by sticks or some other means. They also occupy less space if the plants are kept upright. Many of the peas particularly recommended for freezing grow tall, a factor to be borne in mind. Hazel peasticks are expensive, even if obtainable, so it is well to devise other means. Tall peas can be grown tripod fashion like runner beans, or up netting. For all varieties, bamboos pushed in along each side of a row, with twine or strong thread woven between them at intervals from the ground upwards, are quite efficient and can be used again and again.

The space between the rows

Below: Pears are grown in the same way as apples. Those with a strong flavour are best for freezing. These are the superb variety Doyenné du Comice

Right: A south-west facing wall in a frost-free, sunny area is the best site for peaches and nectarines. The flesh and skin bruise easily so they need handling with care

can be used for quick catch crops in the early stages. Mulch the soil each side of the rows with rotted home-made compost and/or grass mowings. It is a good plan to lay down the latter a week or two before you begin picking. This prevents the soil from becoming too panned down and you will be able more easily to prepare it ready for the crop which is to follow.

Harvesting. If you are not certain whether the pods are full, look at them against the light, when you should be able to see the peas inside. Do not let them become so large that they fill the pod to bursting point, because they are then less sweet. Mange-tout peas should just begin to swell when they are picked.

Freezing

Preparation. Only freeze young, tender peas which are sweet. Mange-tout peas may be frozen while the pods are still flat. Remove ordinary peas from the pods, but only top, tail and string mange-tout pods.

Blanching. Blanch for 1 minute (peas), 2 minutes (mange-tout).

Packaging. Cool, drain and pack in polythene bags or rigid containers. Seal and label. Peas may also be open frozen.

Storage life. 12 months.

Serving. Cook peas or pods in boiling water for 7 minutes, and serve with butter.

Potatoes

Varieties. Like peas, potatoes are divided into three seasonal groups: First Earlies, to lift in late May or June; Second Earlies, for July and August; and Late or Maincrop, for September and October. Recommended varieties include: Suttons Foremost, Aran Pilot (First Early); Majestic, Pentland Crown (Maincrop).

Cultivation. Soil may be ordinary but should be really deep, rich and productive, never heavy clay or waterlogged. Dig plenty of strawy manure or hop manure into either heavy or light soils. Use only a specialized potato fertilizer, no other artificial food.

Tubers for planting are known as sets or seed. Three kilos (7 lb) or so will fill a 15-m (50-ft) row. It is important to buy good seed which is certified virus free. 'Immune' varieties are those which are free from wart disease, a notifiable disease which *must* be reported.

Potatoes generally are divided into kidney and round-shaped tubers. Some varieties are floury, some waxy fleshed. There are also a few special kinds and it is likely that we might see more now that we have the Common Market. Many of the continental 'salad' potatoes, delicious when eaten cold, do not strictly fall into either of the two categories; for example Fir Apple Pink has pointed ends, is elongated and firm.

Seed can be planted from February to mid-March in the South and mid-March to mid-April in the North, but this period can be extended if required. The sooner the earlies are in the sooner the crop can be lifted. Seed can be encouraged to make a start while still out of the ground. Seed potatoes can be bought quite early in the year. Unpack and stand them in shallow boxes or trays with the eye end of the tuber uppermost; these eyes are the buds from which the shoots will develop. Stand the trays in the light in a cool but frostproof place.

Seed may be planted with a trowel; a dibber is inclined to leave an air space below the tuber. The best method is to make a trench about 15 cm (6 in) deep the length of the row. Place the potatoes in this at the correct intervals, 30 cm (1 ft) for earlies and 35 to 40 cm (15 in) or so for the others and place each tuber, eye end uppermost, on a little bed of peat. Sprinkle a few fresh grass mowings over the potatoes, as this is said to prevent scab forming on the skins. Cover them with good, rich soil and then fill in the trench. Rows should be 35 to 40 cm (15 in) apart for earlies, 75 cm (2½ ft) for second earlies and as much as 1 m (3 ft) for the maincrop.

The next important operation is earthing up. As soon as you see the first few dark leaves appear above the soil go along the row with a hoe and gently pull up the soil, first on one side and then on the other, to make a low ridge with the leaves only just visible at the top. Do this from time to time as the plants grow taller, so that the ridge becomes higher and wider, but always leave the leafy part showing. At first this protects the young shoots from ground frost and later it ensures that tubers formed near the soil surface and are well covered and do not turn green from exposure to the light. (Green tubers are poisonous and should not be eaten.) It also helps to keep the plants erect.

In wet seasons potatoes often suffer from blight which renders the tubers uneatable. Symptoms are fading, unhappy looking haulms. Regular spraying every ten days between mid-June and the end of July with a recommended proprietary fungicide should keep the plants clean.

Grow potatoes in a new site each year or let at least two years

pass before you grow them in the same ground again.

It helps to feed the plants while they are growing fast. There are plenty of potash-rich potato fertilizers on the market. But don't overdo it. Once or twice should be enough unless the soil is very poor.

Harvesting. When the haulm or leafy part begins to turn yellow it is time to lift the tubers. Take a full-sized digging fork, push it into the ground at the edge of the ridge, lift the plant and expose the tubers. Pick these off and then fork over the soil in case there are others. Store in the dark.

(1) Wrapping in foil for freezing potatoes which have been baked in their jackets
(2) Heat sealing lightly cooked new potatoes in a boil-in-bag
(3) To thaw, the frozen potatoes still in their bags are placed in boiling water

(4) Packing croquette potatoes in layers with dividers into a rigid container for freezing
(5) Piping duchesse potato mixture on to a baking sheet lined with oiled paper
(6) The duchesse potato pyramids are open frozen, then packed in bags or boxes

Freezing

Old and new potatoes can be frozen in a variety of ways, but do not try to freeze potatoes blanched in water, or plainly boiled old potatoes.

New potatoes. Scrape and grade for size. Slightly under-cook, drain and toss in butter. Pack in boil-in-bags. To serve, put the freezing bag into boiling water, remove the pan from the heat and leave for 10 minutes.

Croquette potatoes. Mash potatoes and form into cro-quettes. Coat in egg and bread-crumbs. Fry, drain and cool before packing in a rigid con-tainer. To serve, reheat in a moderate oven (180°C, 350°F, Gas Mark 4), or fry.

Creamed potatoes. Mash potatoes with butter and hot milk, cool and freeze in bags. To serve, reheat in a double sauce-pan, or use to top meat or vegetable dishes.

Duchesse potatoes. Beat potatoes with egg and butter to a piping consistency and pipe in pyramids on a baking sheet lined with oiled paper. Open freeze, then pack in bags or boxes. To serve, brush with egg and bake in a moderately hot oven (200°C, 400°F, Gas Mark 6) for 20 minutes.

Baked jacket potatoes. Cook until the potatoes are soft, remove the pulp and mash with milk and butter. Return to skin shells, wrap in foil and freeze. To serve, unwrap and heat at 180°C, 350°F, Gas Mark 4 for 40 minutes.

Roast potatoes. Roast in clean fat, drain and cool, and pack in polythene bags. To serve, reheat in the oven in a little fat, or around the joint.

Chipped potatoes. Do not try to freeze raw chips. Cut into pieces and fry in clean fat until soft but not coloured. Drain and cool, and pack in bags. To serve, cook in oil or other fat, or heat in the oven.

Storage life. 3 months.

Left: Rhubarb can be frozen
either raw or cooked. Young,
pink sticks should be used,
washed in cold running water and
cut into sections

Above: Strawberries do best in a
sunny situation. They tend to
suffer from virus diseases, and
only plants certified as virus-free
should be purchased

Spinach

Varieties. Recommended varieties include: Clean Leaf, King of Denmark, Greenmarket and Long Standing Round for summer varieties and Long Standing Winter and Broad Leaved Prickly for winter.

Cultivation. Soil should be ordinary, but moist, deep and rich for summer spinach and rich but well drained and moderately dry for winter kinds.

The leaf beet and the true spinach belong to the same botanical family, but where the first is long standing, the true spinach has until recently been much more of a temporary crop. Indeed, to ensure a succession of some varieties it is advisable to sow seed at fortnightly intervals. However, new varieties have long standing qualities bred into them. One, Sigmaleaf, can be sown in spring or autumn.

Summer spinach takes roughly 9 to 11 weeks from sowing to picking time. Sow from the end of February or the beginning of March in sheltered gardens and so on until August if required and according to variety. Often you will find that a row will continue to be more productive in moist weather than in drought and if it is in the shade or partial shade rather than full sun. Most do best if they are picked continuously. Try to sow rows so that they receive the benefit of the shade of taller plants near them, peas for instance, during the hottest part of the day.

Sow seed in drills 2 to 3 cm (1 in) deep. Rows can be quite close, 22 to 30 cm (9 to 12 in). But winter spinach can do with a little more space, say 30 to 40 cm (12 to 15 in) between rows. Thin out seedlings first when they are about 8 cm (3 in) high, giving each little plant its own space. Return and thin them again when they touch each other and so on until all are roughly 15 cm (6 in) apart. The thinnings can be eaten.

Harvesting. Begin taking the leaves as soon as you think that they are a useful size, but take only the largest leaves from each plant rather than strip it. Nip off the leaves and let the stems remain. These will continue to feed the plant and make up in a little way for the leaves you have taken.

Freezing

Preparation. Use young tender spinach without heavy leaf ribs. Strip the leaves from the stems, and take out any bruised or discoloured leaves. Wash very thoroughly.

Blanching. Blanch for 2 minutes, shaking the basket well so the spinach does not mat together.

Packaging. Cool quickly and press out moisture very thoroughly. Pack in polythene bags or rigid containers, leaving a 1 to 2-cm ($\frac{1}{2}$ to 1-in) headspace.

Storage life. 12 months.

Serving. Cook for 7 minutes in a little butter or dripping, without any water. A little crushed garlic or finely chopped onion can be added during cooking. Spinach can be used for a savoury flan or as a pancake filling; it is also good with poached eggs and cheese sauce.

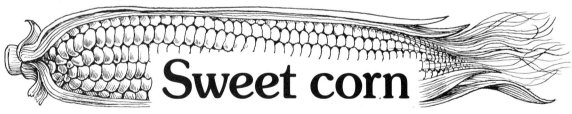

Sweet corn

Varieties. Recommended varieties include: Earliking, North Star, First of All and Early Extra Sweet. Most sweet corn freezes well.

Cultivation. Soil should be ordinary, good, not freshly manured but dressed with a good balanced fertilizer. The site should be fairly sheltered.

Nowadays there are so many varieties of sweet corn to choose from that the gardener must either experiment with two or three varieties each year and finally make his own choice, or simply select from the seedsman's catalogue description. Fortunately, there are good, quick-maturing modern varieties which grow well under our usually not-so-warm summer conditions. Varieties vary slightly in the time they take to produce cobs, in the length of cob, the degree of sweetness in the kernels and in the colour.

When planning the site, select an area out of strong winds. A gentle breeze is needed to pollinate the plants, but high winds tend to blow them about. For these reasons sweet corn is best grown in groups or blocks rather than in rows. This way they pollinate each other more efficiently and also protect each other.

Like most half-hardy vegetables, the seed of sweet corn can be sown either in heat indoors in April, or outdoors under cloches or with some similar protection in May, in which case the soil should be warm and well prepared. The one drawback to growing plants individually in small pots is that they do receive a certain check when they are planted out. This is less likely if they are grown in peat or soil blocks. Another way to lessen the check is to make the planting hole a little larger than necessary. Line this up to soil level with moist peat or well-rotted compost and into it press a flower pot of the same size as that in which the corn is growing. Hold the corn plant steady between the fingers of one hand while you upturn the pot and give it a sharp rap on the rim. This should release the complete root ball. Turn it the right way up and simply slide it into the flower-pot-shaped hole. Water the plant in well, then throw a little more soil over the surface and firm this down.

Sow two or three seeds at a station when sowing directly into the soil to allow for poor germination and do take precautions against mice.

As the plants grow, draw a little soil up around the base of the stems to help anchor them and later when the crop begins to become heavy, place a little more around. Be careful, though, not to uncover the roots; it might be best to import the soil from another part of the garden.

Harvesting. Test the kernels for ripeness by piercing with your fingernail or the point of a knife. If they exude a milky liquid, the cobs are ready for picking.

Freezing

Preparation. Use very fresh cobs with smooth, good-sized kernels, and avoid starchy over-ripe corn. Remove the leaves and silk threads, cut off the stems, and grade the cobs for size.

Blanching. Blanch 4 minutes (small), 6 minutes (medium) or 8 minutes (large).

Packaging. Cool and drain well. Pack individually or in pairs in polythene bags, and be sure to freeze quickly. If liked, scrape the kernels from the cobs and pack in

Sweet corn cobs may be frozen whole or the kernels can first be scraped off

rigid containers, leaving a 1-cm ($\frac{1}{2}$-in) headspace.

Storage life. 12 months.

Serving. Use the kernels of corn in any favourite recipe, thawing for a few minutes first. Corn-on-the-cob must be thawed before cooking. It is easiest to thaw the frozen corn in its wrappings in the refrigerator, before cooking for 10 minutes in boiling water. To speed up the process, unwrap the corn, put in cold water to cover. Put on a high heat and bring to a fast boil, reduce the heat and simmer for 5 minutes. Serve with black pepper and plenty of butter.

Tomatoes

Varieties. Recommended varieties include: Indoors: Ailsa Craig, Big Boy, Seville Cross, Isabelle. Outdoors: Gemini, Carter's Fruit, Sleaford Abundance (bush var.) and Sigma-bush.

Cultivation. Tomatoes will grow in almost any soil, but performance will vary considerably accordingly. Specially prepared soil is best, even when the plants are to go into the open ground. Remove old soil from the planting area and replace with a mixture of four parts good loam (best made from stacking turves) and one part manure or compost plus a little balanced fertilizer. Once the tomatoes are planted and growing well they can receive one of the many special tomato foods.

Tomatoes in pots can be grown in the same mixture or in John Innes soil mixtures or one of the proprietary soilless composts. My own method is to fill two-thirds of the pot with well-rotted manure, cover it with the soil mixture, sit the plant on this and then pack the soil around the root ball. Should the roots appear

above the soil at some stage, these can be covered with a little more soil.

They can also be raised successfully in growing bags, tubular-shaped polythene containers filled with a proprietary soilless compost.

Tomatoes can be grown out of doors or under glass and in heated or cold greenhouses. As you would expect, the latter method results in a longer season simply because the plants can be given an earlier start protected from frosts and given shelter on cold nights when they are fruiting. However, modern varieties of outdoor tomatoes are so good that the beginner need have no fear that this is a crop beyond his capabilities.

Tomatoes generally are grown on the cordon system, which means that one main stem is maintained and all side shoots appearing in the axils of the leaves, except the flowering shoots of course, are nipped out so that the stem does not branch. The exceptions to this are the bush varieties, which behave as their name implies. These plants can, like those grown by the cordon method, be supported by canes to which they should be tied, or they can be allowed to sprawl on the ground. A layer or mulch of clean straw placed under the plants will help to keep the fruits warm and clean.

A row of large pots takes little room and is quite attractive. Often space can be found at the side of a path, along a sunny wall or fence or on a patio. Tie the canes which support the plants to the wall or fence so that the pots are not blown over by high winds.

Tomatoes in containers and in greenhouses need plenty of water, twice or even three times a day depending upon the weather. The soil surface should always look moist, though never sodden. Once the fruits have set, the plants should receive a weekly or fortnightly feed with one of the many good proprietary foods available. Outdoor tomatoes should be protected from potato blight should the season be damp. Spray with a fungicide, beginning early in June and following carefully the directions on the

Tomatoes can be frozen whole without blanching or made into a purée

packet or bottle.

A method which lessens the labour of watering and keeps the plants well anchored (their roots penetrate deep into the soil) is ring culture, which can be used indoors or out. The plants are grown in bottomless containers such as whalehide pots. These are filled with soil (preferably John Innes soil mixture no. 2 or 3), and stood on gravel or shingle, or if available, well-weathered ashes or clinker into which the anchor roots can penetrate.

Seed for greenhouse culture should be sown in early March and that for outdoors in March or April. Outdoor varieties mature more quickly than those for greenhouse culture only. Bush varieties are the quickest, so sow these in April. Usually the varieties which are suitable for a cold greenhouse can also be grown outdoors.

It is possible to sow the seed individually and it is worth while sowing one seed to a soil block or small pot. Otherwise sow in boxes and prick out into individual pots when the true leaves are formed. Do not let the plants become pot bound, but when you see that their roots are filling the pots, transplant them to a size larger. Use a thin cane and stake them early. Keep the plants growing well so that the first truss of flowers is already setting to fruit by the time the plants go outside. Cold greenhouse tomatoes can be planted during late April or May. Those to go outdoors should be gradually hardened off, that is, stood outside during the day and given cover at night as the weather improves. They should be planted outdoors during the first week in June, 45 to 60 cm (1½ to 2 ft) apart. Stake them right away.

Tomatoes planted directly into the soil are not likely to need so much water as those in pots, which should not be allowed to

become dry at the roots. Once the plants are in flower, keep the air around them humid. Spray it at least once a day, more often if possible. The pollen grains will not function properly except in humid conditions, which means that the flowers will not set fruit well. It is possible to use a commercial preparation to help them set.

Harvesting. As a rule the tip of the outdoor plant is nipped out or 'stopped' once four trusses of fruit have been formed. This is to ensure that all mature. If more trusses are allowed to develop, the fruits might remain small and green. These can, of course, be used for chutney. Greenhouse tomatoes can be allowed to develop more trusses.

Fruit of outdoor tomatoes should be picked before the first frosts, that is usually by the second week in September. Well-developed green fruit will still ripen indoors, placed either on a sunny windowsill or in a drawer.

Freezing

Preparation. Whole tomatoes may be frozen but cannot be used for salads, although they are very useful for cooking. They may also be made into purée for freezing. For freezing whole, remove the stems and wipe the tomatoes. To make purée, skin and core the tomatoes and simmer them in their own juice for 5 minutes. Press through a sieve and cool.

Packaging. Pack whole tomatoes without blanching in polythene bags in 225-g (8-oz) or ½-kg (1-lb) quantities. Pack purée in rigid containers leaving 1-cm (½-in) headspace.

Storage life. 12 months.

Serving. Thaw whole tomatoes for 2 hours at room temperature and the skins will drop off. Use them for grilling or frying, or for adding to recipes. Add frozen purée to soups or stews.

Part 3
Fruit

Apples

Varieties. A few varieties can be used as both dessert and cooking apples. If you have room for only one tree and if there are no other apples growing nearby in neighbouring gardens, you will need one which is self-fertile, such as Ellison's Orange or Laxton's Superb, but really all apples do best with a pollinator. This must be a variety which flowers at the same time. Check with your supplier and check also with neighbours if they have apples, so that you and they will get the best yields.

Recommended varieties include: Cox's Orange Pippin, Blenheim Orange (both dessert and cooking varieties), Lord Derby, Bramley's Seedling, Monarch (cook from August, dessert from December).

Cultivation. A deep loam is the best soil for apples.

One feels that every garden should have an apple tree and there are suitable kinds for even the smallest plot. Where there is little space in the open, trees can be trained on walls or fences, they can be used as boundary screens, planted as cordons and espaliers alongside paths and arched over entrances or other suitable places. So-called bushes, pyramids and half-standards take less room and are easier to pick from than a full-grown standard tree, although this can make a beautiful specimen tree for growing in a lawn.

Like most other plants apples are now being cannister grown and can be bought and planted at any time of the year. However, if the plants are to be lifted from the open ground, then they should be planted between November and March. Plants which are to be trained and strictly controlled can and even should be planted much closer than the others. Cordons should be 60 cm (2 ft) apart, dwarf pyramids 1½ m (5 ft), bushes (really trees on a very short trunk) 3½ m (12 ft).

Obviously, culture consists in encouraging the apple tree to produce as much fruit as possible, and this can be controlled to a certain degree by pruning. One should say though, that a large, unpruned tree will still bear fruit. Trained trees, that is espaliers, fan-shaped and cordons, have to be rigorously pruned in order to keep them both compact and fruitful. They are pruned in summer as well as winter.

(Standard, half-standard and bush trees need no summer pruning.) This really is no more than shortening side shoots to 10 to 15 cm (4 to 6 in) during July and August, while leaving the leader, that is, the main stem at the tip, unpruned. In winter these same shoots are cut back to within a couple of centimetres (an inch or two) of their base. This is to encourage the spurs or fruit buds which are always formed on older branches and at the base of shoots of the previous year's growth.

If you wish to grow the trained trees you will need to study pruning so as to get the greatest benefit from them. Ordinary trees need dead wood and crossing branches cut away. Do this quite flush with the main stem.

Harvesting. Apples are ready for picking when the fruit comes away easily from the branch if lifted and twisted gently. The fruiting time varies according to variety.

Freezing

Preparation. Apples cannot be frozen whole to eat raw, but they are excellent for cooking. Crisp apples can be frozen in slices, but those which tend to burst and become fluffy when cooked are better frozen as purée. Prepare apples by peeling and coring, and drop them into cold water with a little lemon juice to prevent discoloration. Slice into twelfths or sixteenths if you are packing slices. Otherwise cook in a very little water until soft and rub through a sieve. Cooked baked apples, crumbles and pies can also be frozen.

Packaging. 1) Mix slices with sugar, allowing 225 g (8 oz) sugar to 1 kg (2 lb) fruit and pack in polythene bags. 2) Pack in rigid containers in a 40 per cent syrup, 300 g (11 oz) sugar to 600 ml (1 pint) water, allowing a 1-cm ($\frac{1}{2}$-in) headspace and filling the gap with lightly crumpled grease-proof or freezer paper to prevent the fruit rising above the syrup. 3) Sweeten purée, allowing 100 g (4 oz) sugar to 600 ml (1 pint) pulp, and pack in rigid containers.

Storage life. 12 months.

Serving. Use apples quickly after removing from the freezer as they discolour quickly on exposure to the air. Use slices for pies or puddings. Thaw purée in the refrigerator for 4 hours and use for making mousses or ices. Reheat purée gently for apple sauce.

A dry sugar pack is the best method of freezing apples, or they can be puréed

Blackberries

Varieties. Modern hybrid varieties are very obliging. Apart from giving high yields, they are varied enough to fruit at slightly different times, so you can select those to suit your convenience.

Recommended varieties include: Bedford Giant, Himalayan Smoothstem, Oregon Thornless and John Innes.

Cultivation. Soil cannot be too rich. It should be a deep, moist loam. Poor soil should be deeply dug and enriched and top-dressed annually.

Although its growth is vigorous, a blackberry plant need not take up a great deal of space. The long 'canes' can be kept under control. You can train them along boundary wires, or wire mesh, or along a fence or wall. If you grow them on a fence, fix wires nearby and not on the fence itself because the weight of the canes might damage it, and in any case all except the self-clinging climbers are best if a little air can flow between them. Train the shoots as soon as they begin to grow. Spread them out fanwise near the ground so that each has its own space, none crossing over another. Tie them to the first wire, which should be 30 cm (1 ft) or so above ground level. If you have enough wires, say five or six at 30-cm (1-ft) intervals, you can take each cane up and along its own wire. If you want to make things really easy in the future, make a double set of wires 30 cm (1 ft) or so apart and then as the new shoots grow you can tie them into place on one set of wires without disturbing the still-productive old canes. As soon as these have finished fruiting they should be cut down to ground level.

If you have a wild area in your garden you can let the plant grow naturally, as a bush, just cutting out some of the old canes each year.

Blackberries are best planted in autumn. The plants you receive will have the canes cut short, but once the roots are growing well, new shoots will quickly be made. They can be planted during winter and early spring, but as you would expect, you will not get much of a crop in the first year.

Once a plant is established it needs little aftercare beyond a good topdressing of well-decayed animal manure or home-made compost once or twice a year.

Harvesting. According to the variety you grow, you can pick fruit in late July and August through to October.

Freezing

Preparation. Use only fully ripe berries that are dark and glossy. Take out any with woody pips or green patches. Wash in ice-chilled water and drain on absorbent paper.

Packaging. 1) Open freeze and pack unsweetened in polythene bags. 2) Mix 225 g (8 oz) sugar with 1 kg (2 lb) fruit and pack in polythene bags. 3) Pack in a 50 per cent syrup, 450 g (16 oz) sugar to 600 ml (1 pint) water, in rigid containers. 4) Crush and sieve the berries and mix 100 g (4 oz) sugar with 600 ml (1 pint) purée and freeze in rigid containers.

Storage life. 12 months.

Serving. Thaw in the refrigerator for 6 hours.

Cherries

Varieties. Recommended varieties include: Morello, Merton Bigarreau (black), Merton Favourite, Early Rivers, Amber Heart.

Cultivation. Soil should be deep, well drained but not too light, nitrogenous, on a site protected from cold winds and spring frosts.

It is important to realize that there is no dwarfing stock on which cherries can be grafted. This means that all grow into large plants, whether they be bush, half-standards, standards or even fan-trained. As you would expect, the latter kind can be better kept under control. Cherries should be pruned very little if at all, so trees cannot be kept small in this way. However, bush cherries are usually neat and easier to pick and spray.

The cooking cherry Morello is usually trained or in bush form and it is also by nature a smaller plant than the others. It will grow on most well-drained soils. Not only will it grow on a north-facing wall and clothe it prettily, but it is also self-fertile. This means that fruit will form on the tree even if no other cherry grows in the vicinity.

The sweet cherries, all of which are self-sterile, are divided into early, mid-season and late-flowering groups. Within these groups some varieties are also infertile with each other, and in order to fruit they have to be

Cherries should be stoned before freezing or their flavour will be affected

pollinated by a variety from another group, provided, of course, that their flowering periods overlap sufficiently for pollination to be possible. Nurserymen give details and advice in their catalogues and lists.

For fan-trained trees prepare the site and establish some means of supporting the trained branches so that they will continue to grow the way they should. A series of parallel wires running at the back of the plant, or a well-anchored panel of plastic-covered mesh will do. The branches can then be tied to these.

The cherries form on the new shoots made in the previous season, so it is profitable to encourage plenty of these to grow. To do this, pinch out the terminal shoots, that is the tips, when these are about 7 to 10 cm (3 to 4 in) long. This will encourage side shoots or laterals to grow. These are sure to be more than you want, and some will be pointing in the wrong direction, if it is a fan-trained plant you want. Tie these laterals to the training wires, none crossing each other. As you work, pinch out those which are in the way. Usually two or three laterals to a stem are kept.

Mulch any type of tree with well-rotted farmyard manure or home-made garden compost in the spring. Alternatively, apply 50 to 80 g (2 to 3 oz) nitro-chalk per square metre (square yard). In autumn apply 25 to 50 g (1 to 2 oz) sulphate of potash per square metre (square yard).

Those plants trained against a wall tend to need a little more attention. They may become very dry at the roots in hot spells, so water them from time to time and give occasional feeds of liquid plant food.

It is helpful to spray cherries in winter with tar oil or DNOC. Alternatively, spray in summer with malathion or dimethoate.

Harvesting. According to the variety, you can pick cherries from the end of June to early August.

Freezing

Preparation. Both the sweet and sour varieties of cherries can be frozen, but the black ones are better. Leave the fruit in ice-chilled water for 1 hour before freezing so that it becomes firm. Dry the cherries and then remove the stones which will otherwise flavour the fruit.

Packaging. Use rigid plastic containers (not waxed) as the juice remains liquid during freezing and may leak. 1) Pack in sugar, allowing 225 g (8 oz) sugar to 1 kg (2 lb) stoned cherries. 2) Pack sweet cherries in a 40 per cent syrup, 300 g (11 oz) sugar to 600 ml (1 pint) water, or sour cherries in a 50 per cent syrup, 450 g (16 oz) sugar to 600 ml (1 pint) water.

Storage life. 12 months.

Serving. Thaw in the refrigerator for 6 hours.

Currants

Blackcurrants and the red and white (the latter is a variety of the red) not only differ in appearance, but they also need different methods of cultivation and pruning, and are therefore treated separately here.

Blackcurrants

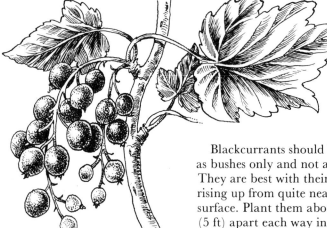

Varieties. Recommended varieties include: Baldwin, Seabrook's Black, Cotswold Cross (for dry soils), Laxton's Giant, Wellington.

Cultivation. Soil should be rich, generously manured, well dug and prepared, nitrogenous and in a sunny situation or between tall fruit trees.

Blackcurrants should be grown as bushes only and not as cordons. They are best with their branches rising up from quite near the soil surface. Plant them about $1\frac{1}{2}$ m (5 ft) apart each way in winter when the soil is in good condition and frost free. Some varieties are much more spreading than others.

It is important to maintain the richness of the soil. In spring it should be fed with 50 g (2 oz) of sulphate of ammonia per square metre (square yard) and in autumn with 25 g (1 oz) of sulphate of potash per square metre (square yard). Meanwhile really deep mulches should be spread around each plant, consisting of whatever materials you may have available, from lawn mowings to compost. These mulches not only keep down weeds but they also help to keep the plants moist at the roots.

Blackcurrants are sometimes affected by aphids. Spray with tar oil or DNOC in winter. They are also susceptible to big bud mite and for this spray with lime sulphur when the leaves are 2 to 3 cm (1 to 2 in) in diameter.

Harvesting. Blackcurrants are most easily pruned as soon as the fruit is gathered. Cut the branches to just below the lowest bunch of currants. Shorten any shoots which did not fruit. If it is easier for you, cut the branches while the fruit is still on them and carry them to a table to strip off the fruit.

Red and white currants

Varieties. Recommended varieties include: Redcurrants, Laxton's No. 1 (early), Red Lake (mid-season), Wilson's Longbunch (late); White currants, White Versailles (early) and White Dutch (mid-season).

Cultivation. Soil should be ordinary but good. Red and white currants tolerate dry conditions better than black. A sunny, frost-free site should be chosen for early crops and late-fruiting varieties can be grown against a north-facing wall.

These currants can be grown as bushes, when, unlike black-currants, they are usually grown on a short leg some 10 to 15 cm (4 to 6 in) in length. Should suckers grow up from ground level these should be cut away.

They also make excellent cordons. These are ready trained by the nurseryman and are usually sold as singles and triple cordons, but they can be double cordons also. They produce larger fruits than bushes. They need not occupy much garden space, but can be trained against a wall, fence or on boundary wires, or against the sides of a fruit cage.

Plant in winter $1\frac{1}{2}$ to 2 m (5 to 6 ft) apart each way for bushes. Single cordons can be 30 cm (1 ft), double 60 cm (2 ft) and triple 90 cm (3 ft) apart. If these are set in rows, leave 1·25 m (4 ft) between them.

These currants produce fruit on the old wood. Prune the plants in February. The leading or main shoots should be cut back by a third, but just tip the leading shoots of cordons. Cut the side shoots or laterals so that just two or three buds remain. If you also prune in summer, in July, you will promote fruit bud formation. Do this by shortening the side shoots to about five leaves.

To maintain yields, apply 2·5 g (1 oz) sulphate of ammonia per square metre (square yard) in spring and the same rate of sulphate of potash in winter.

Harvesting. To reach their full flavour, red currants should be left to ripen for a few days after first colouring before being picked.

Freezing

Preparation. Strip the stems from the currants (a fork is useful to deal with red and white currants) and wash the fruit in ice-chilled water. Dry well. All three kinds of currants may be packed dry, or in syrup, but black-currants may be cooked in a little water and sieved to freeze as purée.

Packaging. 1) Pack dry and unsweetened in polythene bags. 2) Add 225 g (8 oz) sugar to 450 g (1 lb) currants and pack in polythene bags. 3) Pack in a 40 per cent syrup, 300 g (11 oz) sugar to 600 ml (1 pint) water, in rigid containers, leaving 1-cm ($\frac{1}{2}$-in) headspace. 4) Sweeten to taste, purée and pack in rigid

White currants are grown on a short leg in the same way as red currants

containers, allowing a 1-cm ($\frac{1}{2}$-in) headspace.

Storage life. 12 months.

Serving. Thaw in the refrigerator for 6 hours. The unsweetened currants may be used for jam or jelly, and for other recipes. They are good mixed with raspberries and/or strawberries in an uncooked fruit salad. Blackcurrant purée may be used as a sauce for ice cream or puddings, or can be made into a mousse or ice cream. It may also be diluted and served as a drink.

Blackcurrant purée poured over ice cream makes a delicious dessert

Gooseberries

Varieties. Recommended varieties include: Careless (early), Keepsake (early), Leveller (mid-season), White Lion (late).

Cultivation. Soil should be good, ordinary, well primed with sulphate of potash, not nitrogenous because this encourages rank growth, which in turn brings on mildew. Choose sunny, frost-free sites for early varieties. Late varieties can be grown on north or east walls.

Gooseberries can be grown as bushes, but the wise gardener would choose cordons, usually sold as singles or triples, not only because these take less room but also because it is so much easier to pick the fruit from them. Gooseberry plants are very prickly and a really dense bush can be difficult to clear. Plant bushes 1·75 to 2 m (4 to 6 ft) apart each way. Cordons are spaced as red currants, 30 cm (1 ft) for singles, 45 cm (1½ ft) for doubles and 60 cm (2 ft) for triples.

When grown as bushes they are best on a leg or short trunk so that the lowest branches are clear of the ground. This means that the fruit is kept clean and that there is space for hands to go freely under the plant when picking the fruit. Prune to keep the centre of the bushes clear.

Gooseberries are pruned in much the same way as red currants, to which they are closely related. Traditionally they are winter-pruned in November, but where the birds peck at the young buds, this might more profitably be delayed until early spring. Cut back leading or main shoots by a third and shorten side shoots to 2 to 5 cm (1 to 2 in). Those who grow gooseberries for dessert often cut back to two buds only. Cordons are best pruned by cutting all the side shoots to about 2 cm (1 in) in length.

Harvesting. Begin picking the fruits as soon as they are a useful size, usually in June. Make this a thinning process, leaving well-spaced berries to develop for dessert fruit.

Freezing

Preparation. Grade the fruit before freezing, according to size and ripeness. Small irregular-sized fruit can be frozen for jam making. Large ripe fruit will be most useful for making pies and puddings. Top and tail the berries. For a purée, simmer the fruit in a very little water, sieve and sweeten to taste.

Packaging. 1) Pack unsweetened in polythene bags. 2) Pack large ripe fruit in a 40 per cent syrup, 300 g (11 oz) sugar to 600 ml (1 pint) water, working carefully so the fruit does not break up. 3) Pack purée in rigid containers, leaving a 1-cm (½-in) headspace.

Storage life. 12 months.

Serving. Thaw the frozen fruit for 1 hour before putting into pies or puddings. Frozen berries may be put straight into hot syrup and cooked. Thaw purée for 4 hours in the refrigerator before using for fools, mousses or ices, or as sauce with fish.

Gooseberries can be frozen as purée. The fruit is first simmered in a very little water and sweetened to taste

Peaches and nectarines

Varieties. Recommended varieties include: peaches, Peregrine, Waterloo, Dymond, H. S. Rivers; nectarines, Early Rivers, Lord Napier, Pineapple.

Select peach varieties according to where you live. For the North, choose varieties which have finished fruiting by mid-August, such as Waterloo. Southern gardeners can safely choose those varieties which fruit by early September. Nurserymen's lists give details.

Cultivation. Nectarines are a form of peach and can be treated in the same manner, except that they need more water at the roots while the fruit is swelling.

A certain amount of lime is essential in the soil as with all stone fruit, but excessive lime content can be detrimental. The soil should be well drained, not rich or recently manured. A south-facing site, south-west-facing wall and a frost-free sunny area is helpful.

Peaches blossom very early in the year and for this reason alone should be grown where they can be protected and also in places where the early morning sun cannot play on the blossom after a frosty night. Fan-trained trees are easy to protect. They are also excellent for wall culture. Otherwise it is usual to grow bush trees. It is possible to grow peaches in pots and most specialist nurserymen have these in stock.

Support fan-trained peaches in the way described for cherries.

Like most other stone fruits, peaches are best not over-pruned. But of course if the plant is to remain fan trained, those shoots growing out to the front and back of branches will have to be removed to keep the tree on one plane. This is best done in April, May and June by simply rubbing off the young shoots. When the required young growth is 7 to 15 cm (3 to 6 in) long it can be tied to the wires and kept within the fan pattern.

It is possible to distinguish fruit buds from leaf buds. The former are downy and conical rather than round and are obviously to be encouraged. Fruit is borne on one-year-old growths. Shoots which have borne fruit should be cut back each year to make room for new growth. Cut them back to a new shoot as near to the base of the stem as possible. This is the shoot which should produce the following year's fruit. If it grows very strongly it can be shortened and in this case it should be cut back to a triple bud cluster. Try to have the growths for the new fruit 5 to 8 cm (2 to 3 in) apart all over the plant.

As frost is such a determining factor in the success of a peach crop, it is well worth protecting wall plants by covering them at night in February or March. The covering should be removed as soon as it is safe so that early foraging insects can pollinate the blossoms. Yet even so, some artificial aid is advisable. When the blossoms are open, pollinate them with a soft brush or a rabbit's tail, brushing one flower's stamens and passing on to the next and so on. Do this each day for ten days or so, or until all the blossom has opened. When the fruit is about the size of a hazel nut, thin out to 7 to 10 cm (3 to 4 in) apart, and repeat when it is the size of a walnut to about 20 to 25 cm (9 in).

When the tree is fruiting well, give 50 g (2 oz) sulphate of ammonia per square metre (square yard). In March and April apply a good deep mulch of well-rotted manure or garden compost right around the base of the tree.

Peaches become unhealthy from various causes. Die-back is just what it says. Inspect the trees in spring and cut away all dead wood to a growing healthy bud, and to make quite sure, not to the first but to the second bud. Inspect the piece of branch you

Branch of a peach tree after some of the fruit has been thinned

cut away. If there is unhealthy wood under the bud, this will be stained brown, so cut back to a lower bud still, and burn the prunings.

The other persistent and unsightly disease is peach leaf curl. This causes leaves to become swollen, twisted and discoloured. Aphid also disfigures the leaves, but causes them just to curl, not to thicken as well. Against peach leaf curl spray with Bordeaux mixture or lime sulphur as soon as the buds begin to swell in early spring; do not wait for evidence of an attack to appear. Spray with derris or a systemic insecticide against aphids.

Harvesting. If wasps or birds are a nuisance when the peaches are ripening, protect the fruits by slipping the branch and the fruit into a netting tube or a clean plastic bag. The flesh and skin bruises and tears easily, so take care when judging for ripeness and picking.

Freezing

Preparation. Peaches discolour when cut, so they must be prepared quickly. Peel, halve and stone them and brush with lemon juice. It is best to peel the fruit under cold running water, as dipping it in hot water to remove the skins results in browning and softness.

Packaging. Pack in halves or slices in a 40 per cent syrup, 300 g (11 oz) sugar to 600 ml (1 pint) water, with $\frac{1}{4}$ teaspoon ascorbic acid. Put into rigid containers, leaving a 1-cm ($\frac{1}{2}$-in) headspace and filling the gap with crumpled greaseproof paper or freezer paper to prevent the fruit rising.

Storage life. 12 months.

Serving. Thaw in the refrigerator for 6 hours. Be sure to keep the lid on the container as the fruit will begin to discolour as soon as it is exposed to the air.

Pears

Varieties. Recommended varieties: Beurré Hardy, Conference, Doyenné du Comice, Williams' Bon Chrétien, Pitmaston Duchess. Pears are Early, Mid-Season and Late.

It is possible to grow just one pear tree and in this case, Conference or Williams' are the best varieties. Even though these are self-pollinating, they and all other pear trees crop best when another variety is planted nearby. Obviously, the two should flower at the same time. A pear described as Triploid has no good pollen and two other varieties are required to make it crop.

Cultivation. Generally speaking, pears are grown in the same way as apples. Some varieties will tolerate wet conditions more than apples.

Harvesting. Judging the

Conference, an all-round variety of pear which is useful for freezing

moment to pick can be a problem. Generally speaking, colour and size are the best guides: a fruit may feel firm to the touch but already be soft in the centre, and could quickly become overripe.

Freezing

Preparation. Pears discolour quickly and have a delicate flavour, so they must be frozen very carefully. Use strongly flavoured ripe pears, but avoid over-ripe fruit. Peel and quarter them, removing the cores, and dip the pieces at once in lemon juice. Poach the pears in a 30 per cent syrup, 200 g (7 oz) sugar to 600 ml (1 pint) water for 1½ minutes.

Packaging. Drain the pears and cool them, then pack in cold syrup. For better flavour, add a little vanilla sugar, or soak a vanilla pod in the syrup, but do not use synthetic vanilla flavouring.

Storage life. 12 months.
Serving. Thaw in the refrigerator for 6 hours and add to fruit salads. The pears can be drained and the syrup used to make chocolate sauce to serve with ice cream and pears.

Plums and gages

Varieties. There are varieties suitable for cooking and for dessert purposes and there are also early, mid-season and late. Some are self-fertile but there are others which must be cross pollinated. Even the self-fertile varieties crop better when cross

Plums, such as these Victorias, may be frozen whole provided they are not stored for very long

pollinated, so it is as well to have more than one tree.

Recommended varieties include: Early Laxton, Yellow Pershore (cooking), Victoria, Czar, Denniston's Superb, Marjorie's Seedling.

Cultivation. Lime is essential in the soil but this should not be excessive. The ground should be well drained yet moisture retentive and full of humus.

Nurserymen sell all the usual shapes of trees in plums and gages, but one should point out that fan-trained plums really need expert pruning and are not suitable for the beginner. Most plums and gages grow into large trees and need to be planted at least 4 to 5 m (12 to 15 ft) apart, even the so-called bush and half standards. Plums cannot be kept compact by cutting; indeed, they should be pruned as little as possible, with merely the dead wood removed, otherwise they become susceptible to the dreaded silver leaf disease.

Not only silver leaf but also aphids trouble plums. Dead wood should be cut away and burned to keep silver leaf to a minimum. Good cultivation and feeding will sometimes help to cure it. All plums are best fed annually once they have begun to crop well. Give them an annual mulch and to this add in February 3 g (1 oz) nitro-chalk and 1·5 g ($\frac{1}{2}$ oz) sulphate of potash per square metre (square yard).

Against aphid spray with tar oil or DNOC to kill the dormant eggs in winter or with malathion or dimethoate in spring when aphids are first seen.

Harvesting. Plums should be allowed to ripen fully, or their flavour will not be at its best.

Freezing

Preparation. Stones should be removed from plums for long storage, as they tend to flavour the fruit. For short storage, the fruit may be left whole. Wash the plums in ice-chilled water and dry them well.

Packaging. 1) Pack raw plums in polythene bags. 2) Cut raw plums in half, remove the stones and pack in rigid containers with sugar to taste. 3) Cut in halves, remove the stones and pack in a 40 per cent syrup, 300 g (11 oz) sugar to 600 ml (1 pint) water, in rigid containers, leaving a 1-cm ($\frac{1}{2}$-in) headspace and filling the gap with crumpled greaseproof or freezer paper to prevent the fruit rising.

Storage life. 12 months (in sugar or syrup); 3 months (whole raw plums with stones).

Serving. Thaw raw fruit and fruit in syrup for 6 hours in the refrigerator and eat soon to prevent discoloration. If liked, frozen fruit may be put straight into hot syrup and poached for eating.

Damsons

Varieties. Recommended varieties include: Merryweather.

Cultivation. Soil should be as for plums.

Damsons are sold as trees and are not trained as plums and gages are. Cultivate as for plums.

Harvesting. They ripen later than plums, usually from mid-September to October according to the season.

Freezing

Preparation. Damsons tend to be small and the stones are difficult to remove, so they are best prepared and frozen as purée. Simmer the fruit in just enough water to cover, then rub through a sieve and sweeten to taste.

Packaging. Pack in rigid containers, leaving a 1-cm ($\frac{1}{2}$-in) headspace.

Storage life. 12 months.

Serving. Thaw in the refrigerator for 4 hours and serve with cream, or use to make a mousse.

Raspberries

Varieties. Recommended varieties include: Malling Jewel, Glen Cova, Golden Everest, Malling Orion.

Cultivation. Soil should be deep, rich, moist, full of moisture-retentive humus, on a sunny or partially shaded site.

There are summer- and autumn-fruiting varieties. Except for pruning there is no difference in cultivation methods for either of these.

If possible plant raspberries so that the rows run from north to south. Plant the canes singly, about 45 cm (18 in) apart and some 1·5 m (5 ft) between rows. The canes soon send up new growths and the row becomes filled. As the canes grow they should be tied to parallel wires. If growth is very vigorous it helps to make two groups of wires, one each side of the row, so that the canes are not too crowded.

When the new canes are first planted, cut them down to about 30 cm (1 ft) from ground level just above a good bud. After this, all you have to do each year is cut away all canes which have fruited after the crop has been cleared. The exception is for the autumn-fruiting varieties and here all the canes should be cut right back in February.

Raspberries are very shallow rooting, so be careful not to dig around them. Instead, keep a good mulch over the roots. Before the crop is ready to pick spread a deep mulch of lawn mowings on the ground.

Apply sulphate of potash each autumn, about 20 g ($\frac{3}{4}$ oz) per square metre (square yard). It will make all the difference to the size of the berries and the weight of the crop.

Harvesting. When you see that the fruit is well set and just beginning to colour, if water is available flood the rows. This will help the fruit to swell and colour well. Pick the berries when they are dry, for wet fruit turns mouldy quickly.

Freezing

Preparation. Discard any hard or seedy berries. Wash in ice-chilled water and drain well.

Packaging. 1) Open freeze and pack dry in polythene bags. 2) Mix 100 g (4 oz) sugar with 450 g (1 lb) fruit and pack in polythene bags. 3) Pack in a 30 per cent syrup, 300 g (7 oz) sugar to 600 ml (1 pint) water, in rigid containers, leaving a 1-cm ($\frac{1}{2}$-in) headspace. 4) Put fresh berries through a sieve, sweeten to taste, and pack in rigid containers, leaving a 1-cm ($\frac{1}{2}$-in) headspace.

Storage life. 12 months.

Serving. Thaw in the refrigerator for 6 hours (raw fruit or fruit in syrup) or 4 hours (purée). Serve the fruit with sugar and cream, or mix with other summer fruit such as redcurrants. Use raspberry purée as a sauce, or for mousses, ices or milk shakes.

Pruning raspberries. Old canes are cut out after fruiting and new canes tied in

Rhubarb

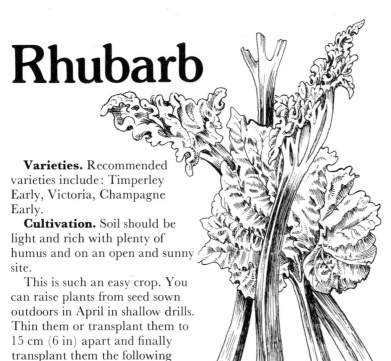

Varieties. Recommended varieties include: Timperley Early, Victoria, Champagne Early.

Cultivation. Soil should be light and rich with plenty of humus and on an open and sunny site.

This is such an easy crop. You can raise plants from seed sown outdoors in April in shallow drills. Thin them or transplant them to 15 cm (6 in) apart and finally transplant them the following winter to 90 cm (3 ft).

Alternatively, you can buy well-grown crowns from the nurseryman or garden centre. In each case you should wait for a year at least after planting before pulling the stalks. Once the plant has become well established it bears prolifically, so give it an opportunity to do so. I suggest that it is worth while to plant several crowns and to pull half or alternate plants and leave the others untouched. This means that when these are really prolific the plants first pulled can rest for a year and then the process can be repeated.

Plant rhubarb with the crowns at soil level. Topdress the soil with well-rotted manure or home-made compost each winter, lightly forking this into the surface. After four years lift the crowns, divide them into smaller pieces and replant.

Do not allow the plants to flower, but cut off the flowering stems as soon as they appear. Pull no stems after about the end of July.

Rhubarb which is growing in the open ground can be forced early in the year, about January or February, by covering the plant in some way, with an up-turned bucket or box or a special rhubarb pot. All daylight must be shut out. When you have placed the cover on, surround this in turn with fallen leaves and fresh stable manure, or failing this with home-made compost – anything to add warmth and to keep out the cold. The stalks should be ready in about three weeks. The plant can be re-covered to force more stalks, but once used this way the plant should be discarded, since it takes a long time for it to regain its vigour.

Roots for forcing indoors are best lifted in November and onwards and left on the ground to be exposed to the frost for a few days before planting.

Simply place the roots close together in deep boxes or plastic bags with a little soil or peat between and put them under the staging in a warm greenhouse, where they can be kept dark, or in a cellar, or even in a spare room, somewhere in a temperature of 13 to 24 °C (55 to 75°F). Water a little to begin with so that the soil is just moist, but as growth accelerates, give water more freely. Slip the boxes inside waterproof plastic bags if you do not wish the floor to become wet.

Harvesting. Harvest rhubarb by pulling or tugging the stem off the crown.

Freezing

Preparation. Use young pink sticks, and freeze either raw or cooked. Wash in cold running water, trim and cut into the lengths desired. To keep a good colour, blanch for 1 minute before packing. Rhubarb may be packed raw, in syrup, or as purée.

Packaging. 1) Pack long stalks of rhubarb in 450-g (1-lb) quantities in foil or polythene bags. 2) Cut in 2·5-cm (1-in) lengths and pack in rigid containers or polythene bags. 3) Cut in 2·5-cm (1-in) lengths and pack in a 40 per cent syrup, 300 g (11 oz) sugar to 600 ml (1 pint) water, in rigid containers, and leave a 1-cm (½-in) headspace. 4) Cook rhubarb without any water, but with a few spoonfuls of raspberry jam; sieve, sweeten to taste and freeze as purée in rigid containers, leaving a 1-cm (½-in) headspace.

Storage life. 12 months.

Serving. Thaw in the refrigerator for 6 hours (fruit in syrup) or 4 hours (purée). Use purée for fools or mousses. Rhubarb pieces can be cooked in water while still frozen, but should be thawed before being put into a pie or pudding.

Strawberries

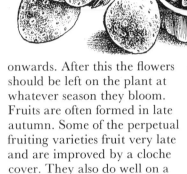

Varieties. There are three kinds of strawberries: summer fruiting varieties or cultivars which produce runners from which new plants can be propagated; perpetual fruiting, most of which do not bear runners, and the small but deliciously fruited alpine strawberries, or Fraise du bois, which are called perpetual fruiting.

Recommended varieties include: Summer-fruiting varieties, Cambridge Favourite, Grandee, Domanil, Tamella; perpetual fruiting, Gento; alpine, Baron Solemacher, Alexandria.

Cultivation. Soil should be rich and slightly acid, with plenty of humus to make it moisture retentive. It should be firm, or if freshly dug should be left to settle for at least a month before planting. Strawberries do best on a sunny site, but alpines like shade.

It is usually most convenient to grow summer strawberries in rows across the garden or along a path. It is also a good plan to grow them on a three-year system, which means that each year there is a young, freshly planted row, one that is two years old and one that is three. When the last has finished fruiting, it is dug out and some other crop put in its place, while the new row is made near the second-year row but on fresh soil. New or maiden plants are used for this purpose.

Late summer is the best time for planting summer-fruiting varieties, season permitting. Perpetual varieties can be planted in autumn or early spring. However, in the year following planting flowers formed in May are best picked off and you should then get a bumper crop from late summer onwards. After this the flowers should be left on the plant at whatever season they bloom. Fruits are often formed in late autumn. Some of the perpetual fruiting varieties fruit very late and are improved by a cloche cover. They also do well on a warm, raised bed.

Should you buy plants by mail order, unpack them as soon as they arrive so that they are in good light. Stand the plants in water for ten minutes and then heel them into moist peat. Place them close together in a small trench with their roots well covered and plant them out as soon as the weather allows, 30 to 40 cm (12 to 18 in) apart with rows 60 cm (2 ft) apart. See that the roots are not cramped and that the crown of the plant rests at soil level and is not buried. Firm the soil around the plants. In winter the frosts sometimes lift the plants from the soil, so go along the rows firming it on each side of the plants with your foot.

Like raspberries, strawberries benefit from a good watering when the fruits have formed. Try to give them a good weekly soaking. The only other time to water is after planting, should the weather be so dry that the plants wilt.

Usually at or about the same

Straw laid under strawberry plants helps to keep the crop clean and dry

time that the plant fruits, sometimes later, stolons or runners are formed. The stems of these are best cut off close to the parent plant unless you wish to produce new plants, in which case leave just one or two runners from each plant. These will root into the ground, but if they can instead be rooted into pots of good soil they can be more easily transplanted later on. Perfectionists take runners only from stock plants which have not been allowed to fruit.

Of the perpetual varieties few produce runners. However, Gento does and these quickly bear flowers and fruit. The best method here is to keep the runners in line with the main plants. These young plants can be lifted and replanted in new soil every third or fourth year to keep the stock rejuvenated. Alternatively, order new stock from the

Open freezing strawberries. Ripe, firm fruit should be used

nurseryman to replace the old.

If you have any doubt about the health of the plants it is best to lift and burn them and begin anew. Strawberries suffer from virus diseases and one should always buy plants which have been certified virus free by the Ministry of Agriculture. Symptoms of virus attack are discoloured, misshapen, curly and crinkled leaves. Aphids also can be troublesome.

Often beautiful red strawberries become soft and mouldy. This is one of the effects of botrytis or mildew. Spray with one of the proprietary fungicides. It is my experience that botrytis is worse when slugs are present, so keep these and snails at bay by using slug pellets. Whatever preparation you use, follow the directions carefully.

Alpine strawberries make attractive edgings to paths and borders. These can be raised from seed and two-year-old plants can be divided. Indeed, they are

more productive if they are divided regularly, say alternate plants in alternate years. If the plants are in good soil, well mulched and watered in dry weather, they can be covered with cloches in early spring and in late autumn to prolong the season.

Harvesting. The recommended practice is that when strawberries are planted in late summer or autumn they can be allowed to fruit in the following year. When they are planted in the spring any flowers which form should be picked off so that the plant can build up reserves for the following year when the yield is likely to be much heavier.

Freezing

Preparation. Strawberries collapse quickly after thawing and become mushy. It is best to avoid sugar when freezing whole fruit as this draws out the juices and increases the flabbiness of the fruit. Use ripe, firm fruit and freeze as quickly as possible after picking, and do not remove the hulls until ready to pack the fruit. Grade the fruit carefully (small berries are useful for jam-making later). The flavour and colour of the fruit is retained well in uncooked purée in the freezer.

Packaging. 1) Open freeze and pack in polythene bags. 2) Pack in a 40 per cent syrup, 300 g (11 oz) sugar to 600 ml (1 pint) water, in rigid containers, leaving a 1-cm ($\frac{1}{2}$-in) headspace. 3) Put the raw fruit through a sieve, stir in sugar to taste and pack purée in rigid containers, leaving a 1-cm ($\frac{1}{2}$-in) headspace.

Storage life. 12 months.

Serving. Thaw whole fruit in the refrigerator for 4 hours and eat while still slightly frozen. Thaw purée for 4 hours and use for mousses, ices and fools, or as a sauce.